it girl
CROCHET

23 MUST-HAVE ACCESSORIES

SHARON
ZIENTARA

INTERWEAVE
interweave.com

editor Michelle Bredeson
technical editor Karen Manthey
associate art director Julia Boyles
cover designer Brenda Gallagher
interior designer Adrian Newman
technical illustrations Karen Manthey
photographer Joe Hancock
photo stylist Allie Liebgott
hair and makeup Jessica Shinyeda
production Katherine Jackson

Interweave
a division of F+W Media, Inc.
4868 Innovation Dr.
Fort Collins, CO 80525
interweave.com

Manufactured in China
by RR Donnelley Shenzhen.

Library of Congress Cataloging-in-
Publication Data

Zientara, Sharon.

It girl crochet : 23 must-have accessories /
Sharon Zientara.

    pages cm

Includes index.

ISBN 978-1-62033-096-8 (pbk.)
ISBN 978-1-62033-128-6 (PDF)

1. Crocheting--Patterns. I. Title.

TT825.Z53 2014

746.43'4--dc23

2013039894

10 9 8 7 6 5 4 3 2 1

contents

Introduction

When I first had the idea for this book, I knew I wanted to reference some of my favorite eras in fashion, but at the same time to create a chic, timeless collection of designs. To me, when an element of fashion from the past comes back around again and again, it's because it can transcend time and trends. The ornate embellishments of art nouveau, bold graphics like those from Mondrian-style dresses of the 1960s, and the flower child sensibilities of bohemian culture all pass this test. Enter any boutique today and there are modern references to all of these eras.

In the same way that fashion has a past, so does crochet. Just as there are references to former fashion trends, crochet influences, such as delicate thread doilies, granny square vests, and motif-based afghans, can be found in many of today's boutiques and even on runways at fashion week. The crochet techniques on these pages all have a part in crochet's history, but I think you will also find that each project will ease you into techniques that you may have been intimidated to attempt in a more complicated design.

I wanted to take the best from the pasts of both crochet and fashion and create something new, beautiful, and exciting. The projects here are handpicked for their ability to be referential, yet timeless in nature—an element that is well worth the time and care it takes to make by hand.

The concept of the "it girl," a woman who possesses a certain quality that attracts others, was popularized in the 1920s and epitomized by Clara Bow, star of the film It, but like fashion and crochet it transcends time. Each generation redefines "it" into a fashionable icon of the moment. Throughout this book, we'll meet a few classic "it girls" and other sources of inspiration for the designs in the collection. No matter which fashion era your inner "it girl" belongs to, I hope you will enjoy making and wearing these projects for years to come.

CHAPTER 1

Crochet NOUVEAU

Fashion frequently hearkens back to the feminine decadence of the art nouveau period of art and design, and for good reason. The colors are rich, the fabrics are lush, and the patterns are bold and intricate. The designs in this section represent the perfect marriage between these sensibilities and modern crochet techniques.

Finished Size

About 20" wide at neck
(56" at hem) × 18" long (51 [142]
× 45.5 cm).

Yarn

DK weight (#3 Light).

Shown here: Madelinetosh
Pashmina (75% merino, 15%
silk, 10% cashmere; 360 yd
[329 m]/3½ oz [100 g]): dried
rose (MC), 2 skeins; moorland
(CC), 1 skein.

Hook

Size F/5 (3.75 mm). *Adjust hook
size if necessary to obtain correct
gauge.*

Notions

Yarn needle; two 1¼" (3.2 cm)
buttons.

Gauge

3 pattern reps and 10 rows =
4" (10 cm) in Pattern 1, blocked.
Motif = 4" (10 cm) in diameter.

Note

*Capelet is worked from motifs
at neck down toward elbows.*

Chrysanthemum
CAPELET

Designer Kathy Merrick saw a chrysanthemum
motif in an old crochet book and thought it had
great shaping possibilities. She originally
intended to create a rectangular wrap, but the
design evolved into a shaped capelet. It's a good
project to learn a bit about three-dimensional
motifs, as the mum is fairly easy to make and
could be made much bigger if you like.

DESIGNED BY *Kathy Merrick*

Stitch Guide

Motif

With CC, ch 4; join with sl st to form ring.

RND 1 (RS): Ch 1, (sc, ch 3) 6 times in ring, sl st in first sc.

RND 2: Ch 1, (sc, ch 1, dc, ch 3, dc, ch 3, dc, ch 1, sc) in each ch-3 sp around, join with sl st in first sc.

RND 3: Ch 1, sc in side of first ch, ch 4, [sc between next 2 sc of Rnd 2, ch 4] 5 times, join with sl st in first sc.

RND 4: Ch 1, (sc, ch 1, [dc, ch 3] 4 times, dc, ch 1, sc) in each ch-4 sp around, join with sl st to first sc.

RND 5: Ch 1, sc in side of first ch, ch 5, [sc between next 2 sc of Rnd 4, ch 5] 5 times, join with sl st in first sc.

RND 6: Ch 1, (sc, ch 1, [dc, ch 3] 6 times, dc, ch 1, sc) in each ch-5 sp around, join with sl st in first sc.

RND 7: Ch 1, sc in side of first ch, ch 6, [sc between next 2 sc of Rnd 6, ch 6] 5 times, join with sl st in first sc.

RND 8: Ch 1, (sc, ch 1, [dc, ch 3] 8 times, dc, ch 1, sc) in each ch-6 sp around, join with sl st in first sc. Fasten off.

Pattern 1 (worked on a multiple of 6 sts)

SET-UP ROW: Ch 1, sc in first sc, *ch 4, sk next 4 sc, (sc, ch 3, sc) in next sc, ch 5, (sc, ch 3, sc) in next sc; rep from * across to last 5 sc, ch 4, sk next 4 sc, sc in last sc.

ROW 1: Ch 9 (counts as tr, ch 5), sk next 2 sps, *(sc, ch 3, sc) in next ch-5 sp, ch 5, sk next 3 sps; rep from * across to last ch-5 sp, ch 5, sk next 2 sps, tr in last sc.

ROW 2: Ch 1, sc in first tr, *ch 4, sk next sp, (sc, ch 3, sc, ch 5, sc, ch 3, sc) in next ch-3 sp; rep from * across, ch 4, sk next ch-5 sp, sc in 4th ch of beg ch-9 sp.

Rep Rows 1 and 2 for pattern.

Pattern 2

ROW 1: Ch 10 (counts as tr, ch 6), sk next 2 sps, *(sc, ch 3, sc) in next ch-5 sp, ch 6, sk next 3 sps; rep from * across to last ch-5 sp, ch 5, sk next 2 sps, tr in last sc.

ROW 2: Ch 1, sc in first tr, *ch 5, sk next sp, (sc, ch 3, sc, ch 5, sc, ch 3, sc) in next ch-3 sp; rep from * across, ch 5, sk next sp, sc in 4th ch of beg ch-9 sp.

Rep Rows 1 and 2 for pattern.

Neck

First Motif

With CC, make First Motif.

Second Motif

Work same as First Motif through Rnd 7.

RND 8 (JOINING RND): Ch 1, (sc, ch 1, [dc, ch 1, sl st to corresponding ch-3 sp of previous Motif, ch 1] 8 times, dc, ch 1, sc) in next 2 ch-6 sps, (sc, ch 1, [dc, ch 3] 8 times, dc, ch 1, sc) in each ch-6 sp around, join with sl st in first sc of Rnd 8. Fasten off.

Successive Motifs

Make three more motifs same as Second Motif, joining each to previous motif while completing last round, skipping one ch-6 space on top and bottom of previous motif.

Body

ROW 1: With RS facing, join MC in first ch-3 sp of next unattached leaf on end motif, ch 1, sc evenly across motifs, working 4 sc in each ch-3 sp, sc in each sc, and 4 sc in each joined leaf of each motif across—216 sts.

Work set-up row of Pattern 1.

Work Rows 1–2 of Pattern 1 ten times. Work Rows 1–2 of Pattern 2 five times. Fasten off.

Finishing

ROW 1: With RS facing, join CC to right-hand side of Row 1 of Body, ch 9 (counts as tr, ch 5), (sc, ch 3, sc) in row-end of first row of body, *ch 3, sk next row-end tr, (sc, ch 3, sc) in next row-end sc*, rep from * to * across to next corner, ch 3, ([sc, ch 3] 3 times, sc) in corner sc,

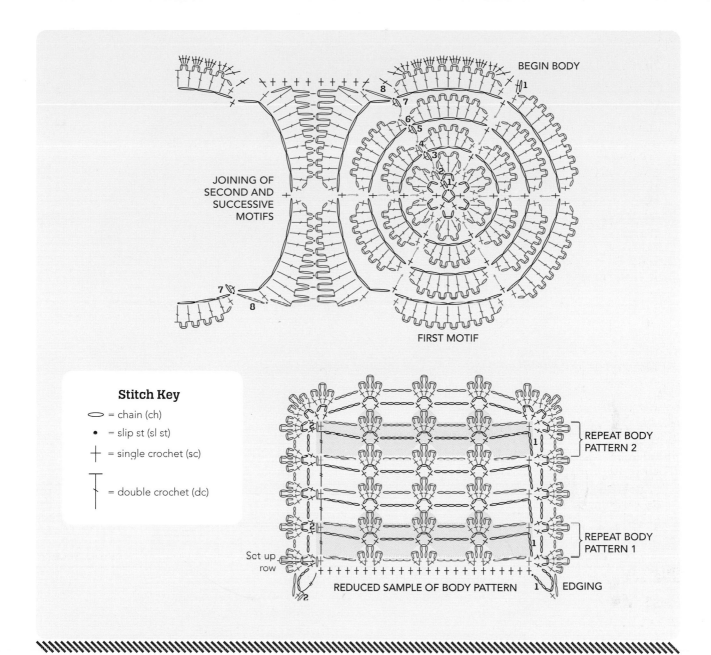

Stitch Key

⬭ = chain (ch)

• = slip st (sl st)

+ = single crochet (sc)

┬ = double crochet (dc)

BEGIN BODY

JOINING OF
SECOND AND
SUCCESSIVE
MOTIFS

FIRST MOTIF

REPEAT BODY
PATTERN 2

REPEAT BODY
PATTERN 1

Set up
row

REDUCED SAMPLE OF BODY PATTERN

EDGING

working across bottom edge, ch 5, sk next 3 sps, **(sc, ch 3, sc) in next ch-5 sp, ch 5; rep from ** across to next corner, ([sc, ch 3] 3 times, sc) in corner sc, rep from * to * across to top of body, ending with ch 5, tr in last row-end sc, turn.

ROW 2: Ch 1, sc in first tr, ch 2, *(sc, ch 3, sc, ch 5, sc, ch 3, sc) in next ch-3 sp, ch 2, sk next ch-3 sp*; rep from * to * across to next corner, (sc, ch 3, sc, ch 5, sc, ch 3, sc) in each of next 3 ch-3 sps, ch 4, (sc, ch 3, sc, ch 5, sc, ch 3, sc, ch 4) in each ch-3 sp across bottom edge to next corner, (sc, ch 3, sc, ch 5, sc, ch 3, sc) in each of next 3 ch-3 sps, ch 2, sk next ch-3 sp; rep from * to * across to top of Body, ending with sc in 4th ch of beg ch-9. Fasten off.

Attach button at each side of neck edge. Use beg and end lps as buttonholes.

Wet block to finished measurements.

Finished Size

Hat measures 24" (61 cm) in circumference; 8" (20.5 cm) deep.

Yarn

Worsted weight (#4 Medium).

Shown here: Dream in Color Classy with Cashmere (70% superwash merino wool, 20% cashmere, 10% nylon; 200 yd [183 m]/4 oz [113 g]): #507 lucky stone, 1 skein.

Hook

Size E/4 (3.5 mm). *Adjust hook size if necessary to obtain correct gauge.*

Notions

Yarn needle; four ½" (1.3 cm) buttons.

Gauge

15 sts and 10 rnds = 4" (10 cm) in Band pattern, sc in blo.

Casa Batlló
CLOCHE

Flappers were the original "it girls," and this flapper-like cloche is a sophisticated piece perfect for any stylish woman. The top circle is built using triangles that flow into each other to create the dome for the head, and the bottom/ side portion of the hat is crocheted as a rectangle. The cloche takes only a single skein of this luscious worsted-weight cashmere blend, so it works up quickly and would make a lovely gift for a friend—or yourself!

DESIGNED BY *Cristina Mershon*

Cloche

First Section

Note: You will make a total of 7 sections.

Ch 17.

ROW 1: Sc in 2nd ch from hook and each ch across, turn—16 sc.

ROW 2: Ch 1, sc in blo of each sc across to last st, turn, leaving last st unworked—15 sc.

ROW 3: Ch 1, sk first st, sc in blo of each sc across, turn—14 sc.

ROW 4: Ch 1, sc in blo of each sc across to last st, turn, leaving last st unworked—13 sc.

ROWS 5–15: Rep Rows 3–4—3 sc at end of last row.

ROW 16: Ch 1, sc in blo of next 2 sc, working across diagonal edge of row-end sts, sc in each row-end st across, turn—16 sc.

ROW 17: Ch 1, sc in blo of each sc across, turn—16 sc.

ROWS 18–112: Rep Rows 2–17. Seven sections completed.

JOINING ROW: At the end of row 112, turn the top of hat inside out, working through double thickness, matching sts, work a row of sc to join last diagonal edge to foundation ch of First Section, turn RS out. Do not fasten off.

Inspiration

Antoni Gaudí was an artist and architect active during the late nineteenth and early twentieth centuries whose work is marked by organic style and references to nature. Casa Batlló is a renowned building located in the heart of Barcelona and is one of Gaudí's masterpieces. The shaping of this cloche reminds me of the rounded, globe-like rooftop architecture of the building. The Spanish tiles produce a painterly hue that gives the same pearlescent effect of this beautiful yarn.

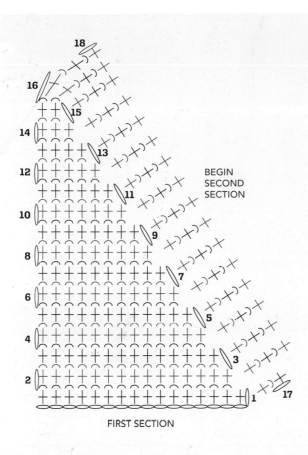

18
16
15
14
13
12

BEGIN
SECOND
SECTION

11
10
9
8
7
6
5
4
3
2
1   **17**

FIRST SECTION

Stitch Key

◠ = chain (ch)

• = slip st (sl st)

+ = single crochet (sc)

⌒ = worked in back loop only (blo)

Band

ROW 1: Ch 1, working in row-end sts around outer edge of Crown, *sc in next 3 sts, sk st, sc in next st, sk sc, sc in next st; rep * around, 8 ch for flap, turn—80 sc; ch-8.

ROW 2: Sc in 2nd sc from hook, sc in next 6 ch, sc flo of each sc across, turn—80 sc.

ROW 3: Ch 3 (counts as dc here and throughout), dc in blo of each sc across, turn—80 dc.

ROW 4: Ch 1, 2 sc in flo of first dc, sc in flo of each dc across to last st, 2 sc in flo of last dc, turn—82 sc.

ROWS 5–14: Rep Rows 3–4—92 sc at end of last row. Fasten off. Weave in ends.

Finishing
Edging

Attach yarn to side of flap, ch 1.

ROW 1: With RS facing, join yarn with sl st in bottom corner of Flap edge, ch 1, working in row-end sts of Flap, sc evenly across, working sc in each row-end sc, 2 sc in each row-end dc, turn.

ROW 2: Ch 1, rev sc (see Glossary) in each sc across. Fasten off. Weave in ends.

Overlapping Flap over other edge of Band, sew Flap to Band. Sew buttons evenly spaced down Flap.

Finished Size

To fit women's glove sizes Small (Medium, Large). Sample shown is size Small.

6 (6½, 7)" (15 [16.5, 18] cm) around knuckles.

Yarn

Fingering weight (#1 Super Fine).

Shown here: Quince & Co. Tern (75% wool, 25% silk; 221 yd [202 m]/1¾ oz [50 g]): #147 wampum, 2 skeins.

Hooks

Standard crochet hook size E/4 (3.5 mm); Tunisian crochet hook size G/6 (4 mm). Adjust hook sizes if necessary to obtain correct gauge. A regular straight crochet hook without a thumb grip may be substituted for a Tunisian hook.

Notions

Yarn needle.

Gauge

28 sts and 28 rows = 4" (10 cm) in sc in blo with smaller hook; 24 sts and 24 rows = 4" (10 cm) in Tunisian crochet with larger hook.

Note

Turning chs do not count as sts, and neither of the 2 chs at the end of a row should be worked into. The reason there are two, and not the more traditional one chain, is to allow a little extra stretch on the upper end of the cuff, adding comfort.

Mes Petites
MITTS

These elegant fingerless gloves have a touch of sophistication that will put the finishing touch on any special-occasion outfit. The unusual Tunisian crochet techniques involved mean they're a bit of a challenge—albeit a fun one—for the average crocheter. Try adding some beads for extra luxury.

DESIGNED BY *Aoibhe Ni*

Stitch Guide

Hand part of Mitts are worked in a variation on Tunisian crochet. At the end of each Tunisian row, draw up a loop in sc on top edge of Wrist, thus joining Hand to Wrist as you go. On Return pass, you will start by working yo, draw yarn through 2 lps on hook, thus joining the last 2 sts together.

Tunisian Simple Stitch (Tss)

Ch desired number.

ROW 1: FORWARD PASS (FWD): Loop on hook counts as first st of Row 1, insert hook in 2nd ch from hook, yo and draw up a lp, *insert hook in next ch, yo, draw up a lp; rep from * across, insert hook in first sc in last row of Wrist, yo, draw up a lp.

RETURN PASS (RTN): *Yo, draw yarn through 2 lps on hook; rep from * across—1 lp remains and counts as first st of next row.

ROW 2: FWD: Skip first vertical bar, insert hook under next vertical bar, yo, draw up a lp, *insert hook under next vertical bar, yo, draw up a lp; rep from * across, insert hook in next sc in last row of Wrist, yo, draw up a lp —1 lp remains and counts as first st of next row.

RTN: Work lps off using standard return pass as for Row 1. Rep Row 2 for Tss pattern.

Tunisian Simple Stitch 2 Together (Tss2tog)

FWD: Insert hook under next 2 vertical bars, yo, draw up a lp—1 lp added. Work standard return pass unless otherwise noted.

Bobble

FWD: Insert hook between 2 sts, [yo, draw up a lp] 7 times.

RTN: Yo, draw yarn through 7 lps on hook.

Right Mitt
Cuff

With smaller hook, ch 42.

ROW 1: Sc in 3rd ch from hook, sc in each ch across, turn—40 sc.

ROWS 2–42 (45, 48): Ch 2, sc in blo of each sc across, turn. Do not fasten off. Sew last row to base of Row 1 to create a tube.

Wrist

RND 1: Working along edge of cuff, Ch 1, sc in each row-end st across, join with sl st in first sc, turn—42 (45, 48) sc.

RNDS 2–12: Ch 1, sc in blo of each sc across, join with sl st in first sc, turn.

Change to larger hook.

RND 13: Ch 1, sc in blo of each sc across, join with sl st in first sc. Do not fasten off.

Hand

Ch 21.

Work 25 (27, 28) rows even in Tss.

ROWS 1–13: Work in Tunisian crochet following Hand Chart.

Work 4 (5, 7) rows even in Tss. Fasten off.

Left Mitt

Work same as Right Mitt through Wrist.

Hand

Ch 21.

Work 4 (5, 7) rows even in Tss.

ROWS 1–13: Work in Tunisian crochet following Hand Chart.

Work 25 (27, 28) rows even in Tss. Fasten off.

Sew last row to base of first row of Hand across top 8 sts, leaving remaining sts unjoined for thumb opening.

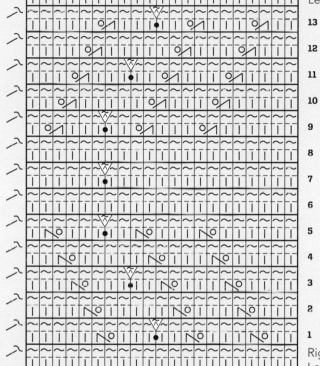

Right Hand: 4 (5, 7) rows;
Left Hand: 25 (27, 28) rows

13

12

11

10

9

8

7

6

5

4

3

2

1

Right Hand: 25 (27, 28) rows;
Left Hand: 4 (5, 7) rows

HAND CHART

Top Edging

RNDS 1–3: Ch 1, sc in each row-end st around, join with sl st in first sc, turn. Fasten off.

Finishing

Weave in ends.

Finished Size

51" wide × 27½" long
(129.5 × 70 cm).

Yarn

Laceweight (#0 Lace).

Shown here: Shibui Silk Cloud
(60% kid mohair, 40% silk; 330 yd
[300 m]/0.88 oz [25 g]): #2012
fjord, 2 balls.

Hook

Size E/4 (3.50 mm). *Adjust
hook size if necessary to obtain
correct gauge.*

Notions

Yarn needle.

Gauge

20 sts and 10 rows = 4" (10 cm)
over Dc Column Stitch Pattern.

Notes

Worked flat in one piece.

Dec 2 sts every row to 2 sts.

*Count carefully to keep track
of decreases, as Dc Column St
should be worked for 75 rows only.*

Block heavily for best results.

Tiffany SHAWL

The double crochet columns of this shawl get
visual interest when worked on the bias rather
than in a traditional vertical or horizontal
construction. The art nouveau–style edging
and the simple base are a perfect marriage
of the fanciful and the subdued.

DESIGNED BY *Jill Wright*

Stitch Guide

Beginning 2 Cluster V Stitch (b2clv): Ch 3, (dc, ch 5, 2cl) in next ch 3-sp.

2 Cluster V Stitch (2clv): (2cl, ch 5, 2cl) in sp indicated.

3 Cluster V Stitch (3clv): (3cl, ch 3, 3cl) in sp indicated.

Double Crochet 2 Together (dc2tog): *Yo, insert hook in next st, pull up lp, yo, draw through 2 lps; rep from * once in next st, yo, draw through 3 lps.

Double Crochet 3 Together (dc3tog): *Yo, insert hook in next st, pull up lp, yo, draw through 2 lps; rep from * twice, yo, draw through 3 lps.

2 Dc Cluster (2cl): *Yo, insert hook in next st, pull up lp, yo, draw through 2 lps; rep from * once in same st or sp, yo, draw through 3 lps.

3 Dc Cluster (3cl): *Yo, insert hook in next st, pull up lp, yo, draw through 2 lps; rep from * twice in same st or sp, yo, draw through 4 lps.

5 Dc Shell (5sh): 5 dc in st indicated.

9 Dc Shell (9sh): 9 dc in sp indicated.

V Stitch (Vst): (Dc, ch 2, dc) in sp indicated.

Dc Column Stitch (multiple of 6 sts + 4, 2 sts dec'd every row)

Ch a multiple of 6.

SET-UP ROW: Starting in 4th ch from hook, dc3tog (see Stitch Guide) over next 3 ch, *ch 2, dc in each of next 4 ch; rep from * across, turn.

ROW 1: Ch 3 (counts as dc here and throughout), dc in each of next 3 dc, ch 2, sk next ch-2 sp, *dc in each of next 4 dc, ch 2, sk next ch-2 sp; rep from * across to last 2 sts, dc2tog (see Stitch Guide) over last 2 sts, turn.

ROW 2: Ch 3, sk next ch-2 sp, dc in each of next 4 dc, *ch 2, dc in each of next 4 dc; rep from * across, turn.

ROW 3: Ch 3, dc in each of next 3 dc, ch 2, sk next ch-2 sp, *dc in each of next 4 dc, ch 2, sk next ch-2 sp; rep from * across to last 4 dc, dc in next dc, dc3tog over next 3 dc, turn, leaving turning ch unworked.

ROW 4: Ch 2, dc in next dc (counts as dc2tog), *ch 2, sk ch-2 sp, dc in each of next 4 dc; rep from * across, turn.

ROW 5: Ch 3, dc in each of next 3 dc, ch 2, sk next ch-2 sp, *dc in each of next 4 sts, ch 2, sk next ch-2 sp; rep from * across to last 2cl, tr in 2cl, turn.

ROW 6: Ch 3, sk next dc, 3cl over next 3 dc, *ch 2, sk next ch-2 sp, dc in each of next 4 dc; rep from * across, turn.

Rep Rows 1–6 for Dc Column Stitch.

Shawl

Ch 156.

SET-UP ROW: Starting in 4th ch from hook, 3cl (see Stitch Guide) over next 3 ch, *ch 2, dc in each of next 4 ch; rep from * across, turn—25 groups of 4 dc.

ROWS 1–72: Work in Dc Column Stitch (12 times).

ROW 73: Ch 3, dc in each of next 3 dc, ch 2, sk next ch-2 sp, 2cl over last 2 sts, turn.

ROW 74: Ch 3, sk next ch-2 sp, dc in each of next 4 dc, turn.

ROW 75: Ch 3, 3cl over next 3 dc, turn, leaving tch unworked.

EDGING RND: Ch 1, working in row-end sts on left side of shawl, *work 153 sc evenly spaced across to bottom point of shawl, sc in shawl point; rep from * across right edge of shawl, sc evenly across top edge of sháwl to beginning corner, join with sl st in first sc, do not turn.

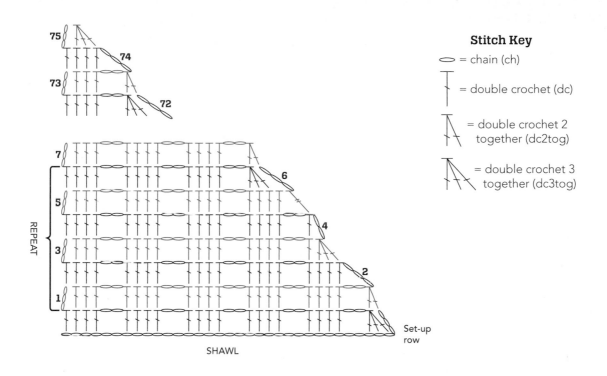

Stitch Key

◯ = chain (ch)

† = double crochet (dc)

⑂ = double crochet 2 together (dc2tog)

⑂ = double crochet 3 together (dc3tog)

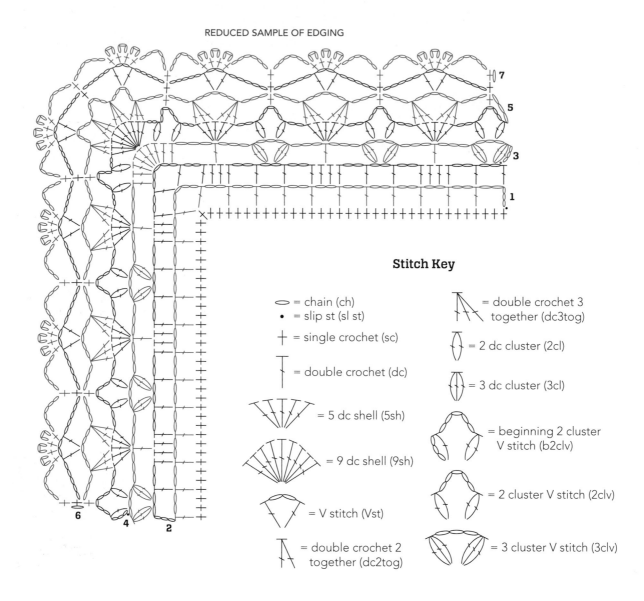

Stitch Key

◯ = chain (ch)

• = slip st (sl st)

+ = single crochet (sc)

丅 = double crochet (dc)

= 5 dc shell (5sh)

= 9 dc shell (9sh)

= V stitch (Vst)

= double crochet 2 together (dc2tog)

= double crochet 3 together (dc3tog)

= 2 dc cluster (2cl)

= 3 dc cluster (3cl)

= beginning 2 cluster V stitch (b2clv)

= 2 cluster V stitch (2clv)

= 3 cluster V stitch (3clv)

Border

ROW 1: Ch 5 (counts as dc, ch 2 throughout), sk next 2 sc, dc in next sc, *ch 2, sk next 2 sc, dc in next sc*; rep from * to * across to sc at center point, (dc, ch 5, dc) in center sc; rep from * to * across to last sc, on right side edge, turn, leaving stop edge unworked, turn.

ROW 2: Ch 5, sk next ch-2 sp, dc in next dc, ch 2, sk next ch-2 sp, *dc in next dc, 2 dc in next ch-2 sp, dc in next dc**, [ch 2, sk next ch-2 sp, dc in next dc] twice, ch 2, sk next ch-2 sp*; rep from * to * 11 times, rep from * to ** once, ch 2, (dc, ch 5, dc) in center ch of ch-5 sp, ch 2, sk next 2 ch, dc in next dc, 2 dc in next ch-2 sp, dc in next dc, [ch 2, sk next ch-2 sp, dc in next dc] twice, ch 2, sk next ch-2 sp; rep from * to * 11 times, rep from * to ** once, ch 2, sk next ch-2 sp, dc in next dc, ch 2, sk next 2 ch, dc in 3rd ch of tch.

ROW 3: Sl st in first ch-2 sp, ch 3, 3clv (see Stitch Guide) in same ch-2 sp, *ch 3, sk next ch-2 sp, sk next 2 dc, dc between 2nd and 3rd dc of 4 dc group, ch 3**, sk next

2 dc, sk next ch-2 sp, 3clv in next ch-2 sp*; rep from * to * 11 times, rep from * to ** once, 9sh (see Stitch Guide) in next ch-5 sp; rep from * to * 13 times, turn.

ROW 4: Sl st in first ch-3 sp, b2clv (see Stitch Guide) in first ch-2 sp, ch 2, sk next next ch-3 sp, *5sh (see Stitch Guide) in next dc, ch 2, sk next ch-3 sp**, 2clv in next ch 3-sp***, ch 2, sk next ch-3 sp*; rep from * to * 11 times, rep from * to ** once, 2cl in next dc, ch 5, sk next dc, 2cl in next dc, ch 2, sk next dc, 9sh in next dc, ch 2, sk next dc, 2cl in next dc, ch 5, sk next dc, 2cl in next dc, ch 2, sk next ch-3 sp; rep from * to * 12 times, and then from * to *** once, turn.

ROW 5: Ch 3, sc in center ch of next ch-5 sp, *ch 3, sk next ch-2 sp, 3cl over next 3 dc, ch 5, 3cl over last dc used in prev cl and next 2 dc, ch 3, sk next ch-2 sp, sc in center ch of next ch-5 sp*; rep from * to * 12 times, ch 3, sk next ch-2 sp, 3cl over next 3 dc, [ch 5, 3cl over last dc used in prev cl and next 2 dc] 3 times, ch 3, sk next ch-2 sp, sc in center ch of next ch-5 sp; rep from * to * 13 times.

ROW 6: Ch 1, sc in first sc, *ch 5, sk next ch-3 sp and 3cl, Vst (see Stitch Guide) in center ch of next ch-5 sp, ch 5, sk next ch-3 sp, sc in next sc*; rep from * to * 12 times, ch 5, sk next ch-3 sp and 3cl, Vst (see Stitch Guide) in center ch of next ch-5 sp, ch 5, sk next ch-3 sp, sc in next ch-5 sp, rep from * to * across, turn.

ROW 7: Ch 1, sc in first sc, *ch 6, sk next ch-5 sp, (sc [ch 3, sc in ch-3 sp] 3 times) in next ch-3 sp, ch 6, sk next ch-5 sp, sc in next sc; rep from * across. Fasten off.

Finishing

Weave in ends. Block heavily.

Inspiration

Tiffany glass refers to the broad range of decorative glass created by Tiffany Studios between 1878 and 1933. The stitch patterns on this shawl remind me of the interconnected panes of glass in so many of the windows and lamps from this era, and the border evokes the sprinkling of intricate flowers that are a trademark design of Tiffany lamps.

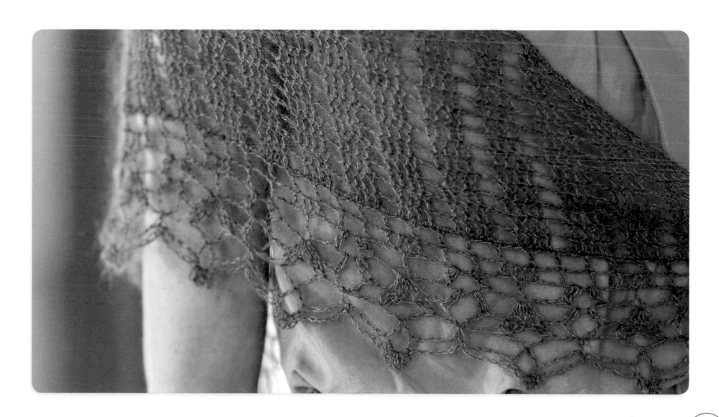

Finished Size

Purse measures 8½" wide × 9½" tall (21.5 × 24 cm), excluding purse frame.

Yarn

Sportweight (#2 Fine).

Shown here: Cascade Ultra Pima Fine (100% pima cotton; 136 yd [125 m]/1¾ oz [50 g]): #3757 zen green (MC), 2 skeins; #3717 sand, #3771 paprika, #3704 syrah, #3752 coral, #3778 lavender, #3753 white peach, #3721 ginseng, #3734 teal, #3744 forest green; 1 skein each.

Hook

Size D/3 (3.25 mm). *Adjust hook size if necessary to obtain correct gauge.*

Notions

Yarn needle; sewing needle and matching thread; ½ yd (45.5 cm) lining material; 5" (12.5 cm) vintage purse frame with matching chain cord; small selection of 6/0 seed beads.

Gauge

15 sts and 12 rows in tapestry crochet, working in blo of sts = 2" (5 cm). Gauge will vary depending on number of colors carried under sts. Overall gauge is not critical, as long as top of bag fits nicely in purse frame.

Notes

Purse is worked in two separate pieces, front and back. Bottom is sewn with sc seam (see Glossary), lining is sewn in place, and then edges are seamed and piece is sewn to frame.

Decs are worked as sc2tog (see Glossary) over first two and last two sts of row where indicated on chart.

(Continued on next page.)

Purse of
PROSPERITY

The pomegranate is a multicultural symbol for prosperity, fruitfulness, abundance, and fertility. It is often cited as a metaphor for a woman's mind—many jeweled thoughts tucked away in hidden chambers. This elegant purse, perfect for carrying your own treasures, is adorned with an image of a pomegranate, worked in tapestry crochet.

DESIGNED BY *Sarah Read*

Notes (cont.)

When changing colors, work last yo of st in new color.

Purse is worked in tapestry crochet with colors carried along under sts when not in use. Do not carry more than two colors at a time over large numbers of sts. For quick color changes, carry up to three strands, otherwise strand third color along back of work, tacking it down with a st every inch. Carry new colors for a minimum of 5 sts before and after that color is used (to secure ends).

Number of colors carried will affect gauge of sts. Steam-blocking panels will help even out any inconsistencies, though fabric will still retain some dimension when finished.

Fabric is worked with RS facing throughout. Join yarn at beg of every row and fasten off at the end.

Sts are worked in blo throughout.

Purse

Front

With MC, ch 64.

ROW 1 (RS): Working in blo of ch, foll Front Chart for color changes, working over a strand of G, sc in 2nd ch from hook and in each of next 30 ch, change to G in last st, working over strand of MC with G, sc in next ch, change to MC, working over strand of G with MC, sc in each of last 31 ch, do not turn—63 sc. Fasten off. (Row 1 of Chart complete.)

ROW 2: With RS facing, join MC in blo of first sc, ch 1, sc in blo of first sc, sc in blo of each st across, carrying a strand of yarn throughout, following Chart for color changes, do not turn. Fasten off.

ROWS 3–55: Work in tapestry crochet in blo, carrying one or two colors, foll Chart for color changes, dec 1 sc at each end of row where indicated (see Notes). Fasten off.

Back

With MC, ch 64.

ROW 1 (RS): Working in blo of ch, foll Back Chart for color changes, working over a strand of G, sc in 2nd ch from hook and in each of next 3 ch, *change to G in last st, working over strand of MC with G, sc in each of next 5 ch, change to MC**, working over strand of G with MC, sc in each of next 5 ch; rep from * 4 times; rep from * to ** once, working over strand of G with MC, sc in each of last 4 ch, do not turn. Fasten off. (Row 1 of Chart complete.)

ROWS 2–55: Work in tapestry crochet in blo, carrying one or two colors, foll Chart for color changes, dec 1 sc at each end of row where indicated (see Notes). Fasten off.

Finishing

Weave in ends. Trim ends in center of work to 1" (2.5 cm).

Steam block bag panels if desired.

Randomly arrange and sew seed beads to center of Front as desired.

Lining

Trace bag panel on lining fabric. Adding ¼" (6 mm) seam allowance all around, cut out lining fabric. Sew bottom and edges, leaving straight section at top open. Hem edges of lining along top opening.

Assembly

With WS tog, join MC at bottom corner of bag panels. Work sc seam (see Glossary) along bottom edge in free loops of foundation ch. Fasten off.

With needle and thread, sew bottom of lining to bottom inside seam of bag panels.

With yarn needle and MC, mattress st (see Glossary) side seams of bag, leaving top straight edges unsewn.

With needle and thread, sew straight top edge of lining to top edges of bag panels using blindstitch (see Glossary).

Remove screws from inside panels of purse frame. Align bag fabric along frame and sew in place with needle and thread. Check that bag opens and closes easily in frame. You may need to rip or sew side seams to get opening exact. Replace metal panels in frame. Attach handle chain to frame clips.

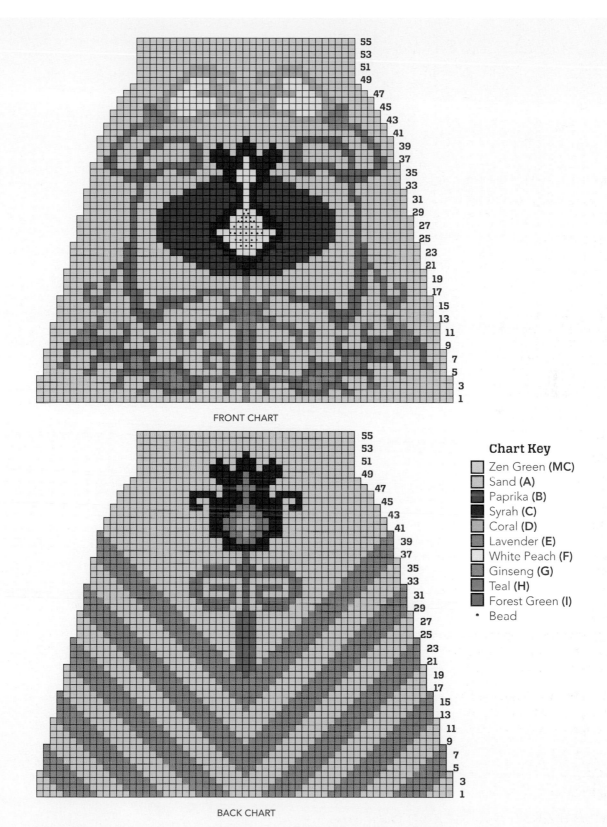

FRONT CHART

BACK CHART

Chart Key

- Zen Green (**MC**)
- Sand (**A**)
- Paprika (**B**)
- Syrah (**C**)
- Coral (**D**)
- Lavender (**E**)
- White Peach (**F**)
- Ginseng (**G**)
- Teal (**H**)
- Forest Green (**I**)
- • Bead

Finished Size

About 59" wide × 29½" deep at center (150 × 75 cm).

Yarn

Fingering weight (#1 Super Fine).

Shown here: Fyberspates Rural Charm 4 ply Sock (70% Bluefaced Leicester wool, 20% silk, 10% cashmere; 439 yd [400 m]/3½ oz [100 g]): pebble beach, 2 skeins.

Hook

Size E/4 (3.5 mm). *Adjust hook size if necessary to obtain correct gauge.*

Notions

Stitch markers; yarn needle.

Gauge

18 sts and 14 rows in solid dc = 4" (10 cm) after light blocking.

Notes

Spacing of decreases in the upper part of the shawl:

The pattern instructs you to space decreases evenly over the row. You might want to use stitch markers to mark the places where you want to make your decreases before you start working each row. Exact placement of decreases is important only for the first and last decrease, which are always worked after the first and before the last stitch in the row. The other decreases can be placed more freely, as long as they are more or less evenly spaced over the row. Take care to stagger these decreases, to avoid visible decrease lines and to create a well-rounded shape.

On Row 1 of lower part of shawl, to work a dc into a ch, insert hook through specified ch. On the following rows, dc sts are worked in ch-sps (or dc).

Shawl GALLÉ

This unique design is a study in unusual construction—it is worked neither top-down nor bottom-up. The circles are stitched first and attached seamlessly, and then the body is worked out from either side. To make a smaller, one-skein shawlette, simply eliminate the top or bottom portion of the shawl. The shimmery silk bits in the yarn make this shawl an eye-catching showpiece.

DESIGNED BY *Annette Petavy*

Circles
First Circle

Ch 4, join with sl st in first ch to form a ring.

RND 1: Ch 3 (count as a dc here and throughout), 11 dc in ring, join with sl st in top of beg ch-3—12 dc.

RND 2: Ch 3, dc in first st, 2 dc in each st around, join with sl st in top of beg ch-3—24 dc.

RND 3: Ch 3, *2 dc in next st**, dc in next st; rep from * around, ending last rep at **, join with sl st in top of beg ch-3—36 dc.

RND 4: Ch 3, dc in next st, *2 dc in next st**, dc in each of next 2 sts; rep from * around, ending last rep at **, join with sl st in top of beg ch-3—48 dc.

RND 5: Ch 3, 2 dc in next st, *dc in each of next 3 sts, 2 dc in next st; rep from * around to last 2 sts, dc in each of last 2 sts, join with sl st in top of beg ch-3—60 dc. Fasten off.

Attached Circle

With RS facing, join yarn with a sl st in 30th st in last rnd of previous circle, ch 19, sl st in 4th ch from hook to form a ring.

RND 1: Sl st in next 3 ch (count as a dc throughout), 11 dc in ring, join with sl st in top of beg ch-3—12 dc.

RND 2: Sl st in next 3 ch, dc in same st as sl st to close previous rnd, 2 dc in each st around, join with sl st in top of beg ch-3—24 dc.

RND 3: Sl st in next 3 ch, *2 dc in next st**, dc in next st; rep from * around, ending last rep at **, join with sl st in top of beg ch-3—36 dc.

RND 4: Sl st in next 3 ch, dc in next st, *2 dc in next st**, dc in each of next 2 sts; rep from * around, ending last rep at **, join with sl st in top of beg ch-3—48 dc.

RND 5: Sl st in next 3 ch, 2 dc in next st, *dc in each of next 3 sts, 2 dc in next st; rep from * around to last 2 sts, dc in each of last 2 sts, join with sl st in top of beg ch-3—60 dc. Fasten off.

Work 7 more Attached Circles for a total of 9 circles.

Upper Part of Shawl

Note: *Make sure that all circles are facing RS up and that the joins are not twisted.*

SET-UP ROW: With RS facing, join yarn with a sl st in 5th st of last rnd of first circle on right, ch 9 (count as tr, ch 5), sk next 5 sts, sc in each of next 9 sts, *ch 10, sk next 9 sts in last rnd of next circle, sc in each of next 9 sts; rep from * until 9 sc have been worked in last circle, ch 5, sk next 5 sts, tr in next st.

ROW 1: Ch 2 (does not count as a st), dc in first st, (dc2tog, 3 dc) in next ch-5 sp, dc in each of next 9 sc, *(4 dc, dc2tog, 4 dc) in next 10-ch-sp, dc in each of next 9 sc; rep from * across to last circle, (3 dc, dc2tog) in last ch-sp, dc in 4th ch of beg ch-9—163 dc.

ROW 2: Ch 2, work in dc, decreasing 6 sts as follows: Work dc2tog in 2nd and 3rd st of row, and in the 2 sts before the last st. Work 4 more dc2tog evenly spaced across row—157 sts.

ROWS 3–24: Rep Row 2 twenty-two times, making sure to stagger the decreases (see Notes)—25 sts at end of last row.

ROW 25: Ch 2, dc in first st, [dc2tog in next 2 sts, dc in each of next 3 sts] twice, dc3tog in next 3 sts, [dc in each of next 3 sts, dc2tog in next 2 sts] twice, dc in last st—19 sts.

ROW 26: Ch 2, dc in first st, [dc2tog in next 2 sts, dc in next st] 5 times, dc2tog in next 2 sts, dc in last st—13 sts.

ROW 27: Ch 2, dc in first st, [dc2tog in next 2 sts] twice, dc3tog in next 3 sts, [dc2tog in next 2 sts] twice, dc in last st—7 sts.

Inspiration

This shawl design started with the background of an art nouveau–inspired portrait—a few lines and a curve of circles that could be perfectly integrated in a rounded shawl. It is named after Émile Gallé, who was a pioneer of the art nouveau movement in France.

ROW 28: Ch 2, dc7tog in next 7 sts—1 st. Fasten off. Pass the yarn end through the last sts once more, tighten and weave in end.

Lower Part of Shawl

Rotate shawl to work across other side of circles.

SET-UP ROW: With RS facing, working in last circle on right, sk 9 sts after the last st of Row 1 of Upper Part of Shawl, join yarn with a sl st in next st, ch 12 (count as tr, ch 8), sk next 5 sts, sc in each of next 8 sts, *ch 20, sc in 13th st after join in last rnd in next circle, sc in each of next 8 sts; rep from * until 8 sc have been worked in last circle, ch 8, sk next 5 sts, tr in next st—2 tr, 2 ch-8 sps, 9 groups of 8 sc, 8 ch-20 sps (250 sts total).

ROW 1: Ch 5 (count as dc, ch 2 here and throughout), sk next 2 sts, dc in next st, *[ch 2, sk next 2 sts, dc in next st] 8 times, ch 3, sk next 2 sts, dc in next st; rep from * 8 times, ch 2, sk next 2 sts, dc in 4th ch of beg ch-12—84 dc, 9 ch-3 sps, 74 ch-2 sps (259 sts total).

ROW 2: Ch 4 (count as dc, ch 1 here and throughout), dc in first ch-1 sp, ch 2, dc in next ch-sp, *ch 3, dc in next ch-sp, [ch 2, dc in next ch-sp] 7 times, ch 3, dc in next ch-sp; rep from * 8 more times, ch 1, dc in 3rd ch of beg ch-5—85 dc, 18 ch-3 sps, 64 ch-2 sps, 2 ch-1 sps (269 sts total).

ROW 3: Ch 5, sk next ch-1 sp, dc in next ch-sp, *ch 3, dc in next ch-sp, [ch 2, dc in next ch-sp] 6 times, [ch 3, dc in next ch-sp] twice; rep from * 8 times, ch 2, dc in 3rd ch of beg ch-4—84 dc, 27 ch-3 sps, 56 ch-2 sps (277 sts total).

ROW 4: Ch 4, dc in first ch-1 sp, ch 2, dc in next ch-sp, *[ch 3, dc in next ch-sp] twice, [ch 2, dc in next ch-sp] 5 times, [ch 3, dc in next ch-sp] twice; rep from * 8 times, ch 1, dc in 3rd ch of beg ch-5—85 dc, 36 ch-3 sps, 46 ch-2 sps, 2 ch-1 sps (287 sts total).

ROW 5: Ch 5, sk next ch-1 sp, dc in next ch-sp, *[ch 3, dc in next ch-sp] 3 times, [ch 2, dc in next ch-sp] 3 times, [ch 3, dc in next ch-sp] 3 times; rep from * 8 times, ch 2, dc in 3rd ch of beg ch-4—84 dc, 54 ch-3 sps, 29 ch-2 sps (304 sts total).

ROW 6: Ch 4 (count as dc, ch 1), dc in first ch-sp, ch 2, dc in next ch-sp, *[ch 3, dc in next ch-sp] 4 times, ch 2, dc in next ch-sp, [ch 3, dc in next ch-sp] 4 times; rep from * 8 times, ch 1, dc in 3rd ch of beg ch-5—85 dc, 72 ch-3 sps, 10 ch-2 sp, 2 ch-1 sps (323 sts total).

ROW 7: Ch 6 (count as dc, ch 3 here and throughout), sk next ch-1 sp, dc in next ch-sp, *ch 4, dc in next ch-sp, [ch 3, dc in next ch-sp] 7 times, ch 4, dc in next ch-sp; rep from * 8 times, ch 3, dc in 3rd ch of beg ch-4—84 dc.

ROW 8: Ch 4, dc in next ch-1 sp, ch 4, dc in next ch-sp, *[ch 4, dc in next ch-sp] twice, [ch 3, dc in next ch-sp] 5 times, [ch 4, dc in next ch-sp] twice; rep from * 8 times, ch 1, dc in 3rd ch of beg ch-6—85 dc.

ROW 9: Ch 6, sk next ch-1 sp, dc in next ch-sp, *[ch 4, dc in next ch-sp] 3 times, [ch 3, dc in next ch-sp] 3 times, [ch 4, dc in next ch-sp] 3 times; rep from * 8 times, ch 3, dc in 3rd ch of beg ch-4—84 dc.

ROW 10: Ch 4, dc in first ch-sp, ch 4, dc in next ch-sp, *[ch 4, dc in next ch-sp] 4 times, ch 3, dc in next ch-sp, [ch 4, dc in next ch-sp] 4 times; rep from * 8 times, ch 1, dc in 3rd ch of beg ch-6—85 dc.

ROW 11: Ch 7 (count as dc, ch 4 here and throughout), sk next ch-1 sp, dc in next ch-sp, *ch 5, dc in next ch-sp, [ch 4, dc in next ch-sp] 7 times, ch 5, dc in next ch-sp; rep from * 8 times, ch 4, dc in 3rd ch of beg ch-4—84 dc.

ROW 12: Ch 5, dc in first ch-1 sp, ch 4, dc in next ch-sp, *[ch 5, dc in next ch-sp] twice, [ch 4, dc in next ch-sp) 5 times, [ch 5, dc in next ch-sp] twice; rep from * 8 times, ch 2, dc in 3rd ch of beg ch-7—85 dc.

ROW 13: Ch 7, sk ch-1 sp, dc in next ch-sp, *[ch 5, dc in next ch-sp] 3 times, [ch 4, dc in next ch-sp] 3 times, [ch 5, dc in next ch-sp] 3 times; rep from * 8 times, ch 4, dc in 3rd ch of beg ch-5—84 dc.

ROW 14: Ch 5, dc in first ch-sp, ch 4, dc in next ch-sp, *[ch 5, dc in next ch-sp] 4 times, ch 4, dc in next ch-sp, [ch 5, dc in next ch-sp] 4 times; rep from * 8 times, ch 2, dc in 3rd ch of beg ch-7—85 dc.

ROW 15: Ch 8 (count as dc, ch 5 here and throughout), sk next ch-1 sp, dc in next ch-sp, *ch 6, dc in next ch-sp, [ch 5, dc in next ch-sp] 7 times, ch 6, dc in next ch-sp; rep from * 8 times, ch 5, dc in 3rd ch of beg ch-5—84 dc.

ROW 16: Ch 5, dc in first ch-sp, ch 5, dc in next ch-sp, *[ch 6, dc in next ch-sp] twice, [ch 5, dc in next ch-sp] 5 times, [ch 6, dc in next ch-sp] twice; rep from * 8 times, ch 2, dc in 3rd ch of beg ch-8—85 dc.

ROW 17: Ch 8, sk next ch-1 sp, dc in next ch-sp, *[ch 6, dc in next ch-sp] 3 times, [ch 5, dc in next ch-sp] 3 times, [ch 6, dc in next ch-sp] 3 times; rep from * 8 times, ch 5, dc in 3rd ch of beg ch-5—84 dc.

ROW 18: Ch 5, dc in first ch-sp, ch 5, dc in next ch-sp, *[ch 6, dc in next ch-sp] 4 times, ch 5, dc in next ch-sp, [ch 6, dc in next ch-sp] 4 times; rep from * 8 times, ch 2, dc in 3rd ch of beg ch-8—85 dc.

ROW 19: Ch 9 (count as dc, ch 6 here and throughout), sk next ch-1 sp, dc in next ch-sp, *ch 7, dc in next ch-sp, [ch 6, dc in next ch-sp] 7 times, ch 7, dc in next ch-sp; rep from * 8 times, ch 6, dc in 3rd ch of beg ch-5—84 dc.

ROW 20: Ch 6, dc in first ch-sp, ch 6, dc in next ch-sp, *[ch 7, dc in next ch-sp] twice, [ch 6, dc in next ch-sp] 5 times, [ch 7, dc in next ch-sp] twice; rep from * 8 times, ch 3, dc in 3rd ch of beg ch-9—85 dc.

ROW 21: Ch 9, sk next ch-1 sp, dc in next ch-sp, *[ch 7, dc in next ch-sp] 3 times, [ch 6, dc in next ch-sp] 3 times, [ch 7, dc in next ch-sp] 3 times; rep from * 8 times, ch 6, dc in 3rd ch of beg ch-6—84 dc.

ROW 22: Ch 6, dc in first ch-sp, ch 6, dc in next ch-sp, *[ch 7, dc in next ch-sp] 4 times, ch 6, dc in next ch-sp, [ch 7, dc in next ch-sp] 4 times; rep from * 8 times, ch 3, dc in 3rd ch of beg ch-5—85 dc.

ROW 23: Ch 9, sk next ch-1 sp, dc in next ch-sp, *ch 8, dc in next ch-sp, [ch 7, dc in next ch-sp] 7 times, ch 8, dc in next ch-sp; rep from * 8 times, ch 6, dc in 3rd ch of beg ch-6—84 dc.

ROW 24: Ch 6, dc in first ch-sp, ch 7, dc in next ch-sp, *[ch 8, dc in next ch-sp] twice, [ch 7, dc in next ch-sp] 5 times, [ch 8, dc in next ch-sp] twice; rep from * 8 times, ch 3, dc in 3rd ch of beg ch-9—85 dc.

ROW 25: Ch 10 (count as dc, ch 7 here and throughout), sk next ch-1 sp, dc in next ch-sp, *[ch 8, dc in next ch-sp] 3 times, [ch 7, dc in next ch-sp] 3 times, [ch 8, dc in next ch-sp] 3 times; rep from * 8 times, ch 7, dc in 3rd ch of beg ch-6—84 dc.

ROW 26: Ch 6, dc in first ch-sp, ch 7, dc in next ch-sp, *[ch 8, dc in next ch-sp] 4 times, ch 7, dc in next ch-sp, [ch 8, dc in next ch-sp] 4 times; rep from * 8 times, ch 3, dc in 3rd ch of beg ch-10—85 dc.

ROW 27: Ch 10, sk next ch-1 sp, dc in next ch-sp, *ch 9, dc in next ch-sp, [ch 8, dc in next ch-sp] 7 times, ch 9, dc in next ch-sp; rep from * 8 times, ch 7, dc in 3rd ch of beg ch-6—84 dc.

ROW 28: Ch 6, dc in first ch-sp, ch 8, dc in next ch-sp, *[ch 9, dc in next ch-sp] twice, [ch 8, dc in next ch-sp] 5 times, [ch 9, dc in next ch-sp] twice; rep from * 8 times, ch 3, dc in 3rd ch of beg ch-10—85 dc.

ROW 29: Ch 11 (count as dc, ch 8 here and throughout), sk next ch-1 sp, dc in next ch-sp, *[ch 9, dc in next ch-sp] 3 times, [ch 8, dc in next ch-sp] 3 times, [ch 9, dc in next

it girl CROCHET

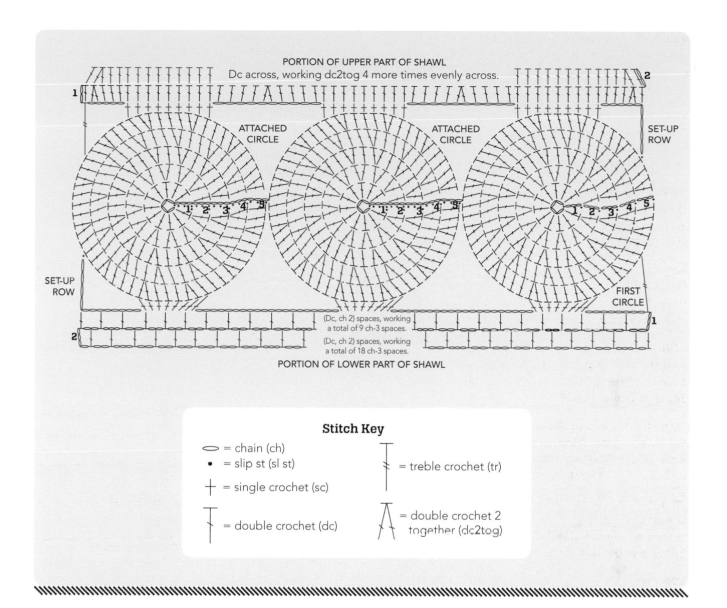

PORTION OF UPPER PART OF SHAWL
Dc across, working dc2tog 4 more times evenly across.

ATTACHED CIRCLE

ATTACHED CIRCLE

SET-UP ROW

SET-UP ROW

FIRST CIRCLE

(Dc, ch 2) spaces, working a total of 9 ch-3 spaces.

(Dc, ch 2) spaces, working a total of 18 ch-3 spaces.

PORTION OF LOWER PART OF SHAWL

Stitch Key

⬯ = chain (ch)

• = slip st (sl st)

✝ = single crochet (sc)

⊤ = double crochet (dc)

⸸ = treble crochet (tr)

⋀ = double crochet 2 together (dc2tog)

ch-sp] 3 times; rep from * 8 times, ch 8, dc in 3rd ch of beg ch-6—84 dc.

ROW 30: Ch 7 (count as dc, ch 4), dc in first ch-sp, ch 8, dc in next ch-sp, *[ch 9, dc in next ch-sp] 4 times, ch 8, dc in next ch-sp, [ch 9, dc in next ch-sp] 4 times; rep from * 8 times, ch 4, dc in 3rd ch of beg ch-11—85 dc.

ROW 31: Ch 11 (count as dc, ch 8), sk next ch-1 sp, dc in next ch-sp, *ch 10, dc in next ch-sp, [ch 9, dc in next ch-sp] 7 times, ch 10, dc in next ch-sp; rep from * 8 times, ch 8, dc in 3rd ch of beg ch-7—84 dc.

ROW 32: Ch 1 (does not count as a st), sc in first dc, 8 sc in next ch-sp, *10 sc in next ch-10 sp, 9 sc in each of next 7 ch-9 sps, 10 sc in next ch-sp; rep from * 8 times, 8 sc in last ch-sp, sc in 3rd ch of beg ch-11—765 sc.

Finishing

Weave in ends. Block lightly. Do not pull too hard when blocking to avoid distorting the circles.

Finished Size

70" wide × 26" long
(178 × 66 cm). The size of the
shawl can be adjusted in 8-row
increments of the main pattern.

Yarn

Laceweight (#0 Lace).

Shown here: Malabrigo Lace
(100% baby merino wool; 470 yd
[430 m]/1¾ oz [50 g]): #9 polar
morn (MC), #62 marine (CC),
1 skein each.

Hook

Size G/6 (4 mm). *Adjust hook
size if necessary to obtain correct
gauge.*

Notions

Yarn needle.

Gauge

First 2 rows of shawl pattern =
3" (7.5 cm) wide × 1¼" (3.2 cm)
tall. 2 reps in shawl pattern =
3½" (9 cm), 11 rows = 4" (10 cm)
blocked. Gauge is not critical.

Note

*The shawl is worked in rows from
center out.*

Shawl VIGNE

This versatile shawl has a traditional shape but
is made modern with the addition of a second
color. Adventurous crocheters could create a
different border using Irish crochet or
Romanian cord crochet techniques for a lush
free-form frame. The main body stitch pattern
is easily memorized, making this a great
on-the-go project.

DESIGNED BY *Natasha Robarge*

Stitch Guide

2-dc Cluster (2-dc cl): Yo, insert hook in indicated stitch, yo and pull up lp, [yo, draw through two loops] twice, yo, draw through all lps on hook.

4-dc Cluster (4-dc cl): [Yo, insert hook in indicated st, yo and pull up lp, yo, draw through two lps] 4 times, yarn over, draw through all lps on hook.

Petal: (2-dc cl, ch 3, sl st, ch 3, 2-dc cl, ch 3, sl st, ch 3, 2-dc cl) in same st.

Picot: Ch 3, sl st under two front strands at the top of the dc just made.

Inspiration

This shawl was inspired by photographs of art nouveau decorative panels with their juxtaposition of geometric and floral motifs. The designer's original vision was to create a piece with diamonds or circles inside a structured frame of free-form vines. The final shawl is an adapted version of that vision with simplified and repeatable stitch patterns.

Shawl

With MC, ch 7.

ROW 1: 2 dc in 5th ch from hook, (2 dc, ch 1, 2 dc) in next ch, (2 dc, tr) in last ch, turn. (Beg ch-4 counts as tr).

ROW 2: Ch 4, 3 dc in first tr, dc in each of next 4 dc, (dc, ch 3, dc) in center ch-1 sp, dc in next 4 dc, (3 dc, tr) in top of beg ch, turn.

ROW 3: Ch 7 (counts as tr, ch 3 here and throughout), sc in first tr, ch 1, sk next dc, sc in next dc, ch 3, sk next 2 dc, dc in next dc, ch 3, sk next 2 dc, sc in next dc, ch 1, (sc, ch 1, sc, ch 1, sc) in center ch-3 sp, ch 1, sc in next dc, ch 3, sk next 2 dc, dc in next dc, ch 3, sk next 2 dc, sc in next dc, ch 1, sk next dc, (sc, ch 3, tr) in top of beg ch, turn.

ROW 4: Ch 1, sc in first tr, ch 1, sc in next ch-3 sp, *ch 3, dc in next ch-1 sp, ch 3, sc in next ch-3 sp, ch 1, sc in next ch-3 sp*; rep from * to * across to last ch-3 sp before center, ch 3, dc in next ch-1 sp, ch 3, sc in next ch-1 sp, ch 1, sc in next ch-1 sp (center ch-1 sp made); rep from * to * across, ending with last sc in 4th ch of beg ch-7, turn.

ROW 5: Ch 7, *dc in next ch-1 sp, ch 3, sc in next ch-3 sp, ch 1, sc in next ch-3 sp, ch 3*; rep from * to * across to center, (dc, ch 3, dc, ch 3, dc) in center ch-1 sp, **ch 3, sc in next ch-3 sp, ch 1, sc in next ch-3 sp, ch 3, dc in next ch-1 sp, ch 3; rep from ** across to last ch-1 sp, ch 3, tr in last sc, turn.

ROW 6: Ch 7, dc in first tr, ch 3, sc in next ch-3 sp, ch 1, sc in next ch-3 sp, *ch 3, dc in next ch-1 sp, ch 3, sc in next ch-3 sp, ch 1, sc in next ch-3 sp*; rep from * to * across last ch-3 sp before center dc, ch 3, sk center dc, ch 1, sc in next ch-3 sp; rep from * to * across to last ch-3 sp, ch 3, (dc, ch 3, tr) in 4th ch of beg ch-7, turn.

ROW 7: Ch 7, *sc in next ch-3 sp, ch 1, sc in next ch-3 sp, ch 3, dc in next ch-1 sp, ch 3; rep from * to * across to center ch-3 sp, (sc, ch 1, sc) in center ch-3 sp, ch 3, dc in next ch-1 sp, ch 3; rep from * to * across to last 2 ch-3 sps, sc in next ch-3 sp, ch 2, sc in next ch-3 sp, tr in 4th ch of beg ch-7 sp, turn.

ROW 8: Ch 1, sc in first tr, ch 1, *sc in next ch-3 sp, ch 3, dc in next ch-1 sp, ch 3, sc in next ch-3 sp, ch 1; rep from * across to last ch-3 sp, sc in 4th ch of beg ch-7, turn.

ROW 9: Ch 7, *dc in next ch-1 sp, ch 3, sc in next ch-3 sp, ch 1, sc in next ch-3 sp, ch 3; rep from * across to last ch-1 sp, dc in last ch-1 sp, ch 3, tr in last sc, turn.

ROW 10: Ch 7, dc in first tr, ch 3, sc in next ch-3 sp, ch 1, sc in next ch-3 sp, *ch 3, dc in next ch-1 sp, ch 3, sc in next ch-3 sp, ch 1, sc in next ch-3 sp*; rep from * to * across to last ch-3 sp before center ch-3 sp, ch 3, (dc, ch 3, dc) in center ch-1 sp, ch 3, sc in next ch-3 sp, ch 1, sc in next ch-3 sp; rep from * to * across to last ch-3 sp, ch 3, (dc, ch 3, tr) in 4th ch of beg ch-7, turn.

ROW 11: Ch 7, *sc in next ch-3 sp, ch 1, sc in next ch-3 sp, ch 3, dc in next ch-1 sp, ch 3*; rep from * to * across to last ch-1 sp before center, sc in next ch-3 sp, ch 1, (sc, ch 1, sc, ch 1, sc) in center ch-3 sp, ch 1, sc in next ch-3 sp, ch 3, dc in next ch-1 sp, ch 3; rep from * across to last

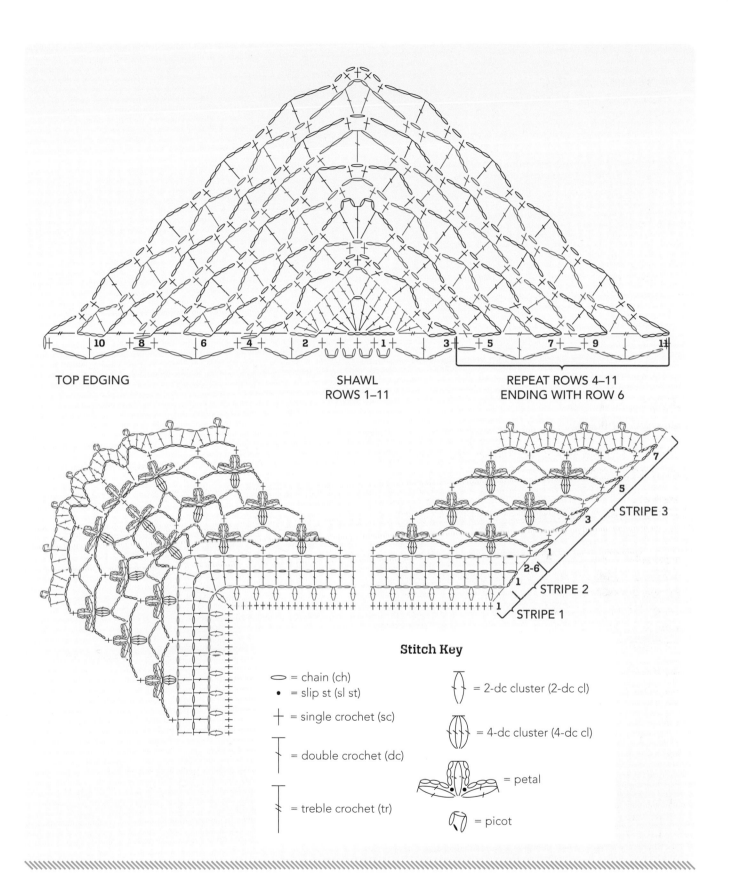

TOP EDGING

SHAWL
ROWS 1–11

REPEAT ROWS 4–11
ENDING WITH ROW 6

STRIPE 3

STRIPE 2

STRIPE 1

Stitch Key

$\bigcirc$ = chain (ch)

$\bullet$ = slip st (sl st)

$+$ = single crochet (sc)

$\mid$ = double crochet (dc)

$\not\mid$ = treble crochet (tr)

ϕ = 2-dc cluster (2-dc cl)

ϕ = 4-dc cluster (4-dc cl)

= petal

= picot

ch-1 sp, sc in next ch-3 sp, ch 1, sc in next ch-3 sp, ch 3, tr in 4th ch of beg ch-7, turn.

ROWS 12–46: Rep Rows 4–11 (4 times); then rep Rows 4–6 once.

Note: *To adjust shawl size, change the number of reps.*

Do not turn. Continue along the top of the triangle working only in sps created by ch-7 or tr.

Top Edging

Sc in first row-end tr, *ch 3, dc in next row-end tr, ch 3**, sc in next row-end tr, ch 1, sc in next row-end tr*; rep from * to * across to center, ending last rep at ** with last dc in row-end tr of Row 2, (sc, ch 3, sc) in next row-end tr, ch 3, sc in center ch, ch 3, (sc, ch 3, sc) in next row-end tr; rep from * to * across, ending last rep at **, sc top of last ch-4 sp. This row gathers the top edge a bit and will help to neatly block it. Join CC yarn to last sc. Do not turn. Do not break MC yarn.

Stripe 1

ROW 1: With CC, ch 1, *4 sc in each of next 2 ch-3 sps**, sc in next ch-1 sp; rep from * across to center ch-3 sp, 3 sc in center ch-3 sp, sc in next ch-1 sp; rep from * to * across, ending last rep at **, turn.

ROW 2: Ch 6 (counts as tr, ch 2), 2-dc cl in first sc, *ch 2, sk next 2 sc, 2-dc cl in next sc*; rep from * to * across to center sc, ch 2, 2-dc cl in center sc, ch 2, 2-dc cl in next sc; rep from * to * across, ending with (2-dc cl, ch 2, tr) in last sc, turn. Join MC in tr. Fasten off CC.

Stripe 2

Note: *In Row 1 count all sts (ch and 2-dc cls); work in sts not in sps. Here and further in the pattern, insert hook under two strands when working in ch sts.*

ROW 1: With MC, ch 5 (counts as tr, ch 1 here and throughout), dc in first tr, *ch 1, sk 1 st, dc in next st*; rep from * to * across last 2-dc cl before center, ch 1, (dc, ch 3, dc) in center 2-dc cl; rep from * to * across to last 2-dc cl, ch 1, (dc, ch 1, tr) in 4th ch of beg ch-5, turn.

ROWS 2–6: Ch 5, dc in first tr, *ch 1, dc in next dc; rep from * to * across last dc before center ch-3 sp, ch 1, (dc, ch 3, dc) in center ch-3 sp; rep from * across to last dc, ch 1, (dc, ch 1, tr) in 4th ch of beg ch-5, turn. Join CC in tr. Fasten off MC.

Stripe 3

With CC, ch 8 (counts as tr, ch 4 here and throughout), sc in first tr, *ch 7, sk next 2 dc, 4-dc cl in next dc, ch 7, sk next 2 dc, sc in next dc*; rep from * to * across to center, omitting last sc, (sc, ch 7, 4-dc cl, ch 7, sc) in center ch-3 sp; rep from * to * across, ending with (last sc, ch 4, tr) in 4th ch of beg ch-5, turn.

ROW 2: Ch 8, sc in next ch-4 sp, *ch 7, sl st in 4th ch of next ch-7 sp, petal in next 4-dc cl**, sl st in 4th ch of next ch-7 sp; rep from * across, ending last rep at **, sc in last ch-4 sp, ch 4, tr in 4th ch of beg ch-8, turn.

ROW 3: Ch 8, sc in first ch-4 sp, *ch 7, 4-dc cl in 4th ch of next ch-7 sp, ch 7**, sc in center 2-dc cl of next petal; rep from * to * across to center petal, sc in top of first 2-dc cl of center petal, ch 7, 4-dc cl in next 2-dc cl, ch 7, sc in next 2-dc cl of center petal; rep from * to * across, ending last rep at **, sc in last ch-4 sp, ch 4, tr in 4th ch of beg ch-8, turn.

ROW 4: Ch 8, sc in first ch-4 sp, *ch 7, sl st in 4th ch of next ch-7, petal in next 4-dc cl, sl st in 4th ch of next ch-7; rep from * across to last ch-7 sp, ch 7, sc in last ch-4 sp, ch 4, tr in 4th ch of beg ch-8, turn.

ROW 5: Ch 8, sc in first ch-4 sp, *ch 7, 4-dc cl in 4th ch of next ch-7, ch 7**, sc in center 2-dc cl of next petal; rep from * across, ending last rep at **, sc in last ch-4 sp, ch 4, tr in 4th ch of beg ch-8, turn.

ROW 6: Ch 8, sc in first ch-4 sp, *ch 7, sl st in 4th ch of next ch-7, petal in next 4-dc cl, sl st in 4th ch of next ch-7*; rep from * across to ch-7 sp before center sc, working ch-7, work petal in center sc, sl st in 4th ch of next ch-7, without working ch-7, work petal in next 4-dc cl, sl st in 4th ch of next ch-7; rep from * to * across to last ch-7 sp, ch 7, sc in last ch-4 sp, ch 4, tr in 4th ch of beg ch-8, turn.

ROW 7: Ch 8, sc in first ch-4 sp, *ch 7, sc in next ch-7 sp, ch 7**, sc in center 2-dc cl of next petal*; rep from * to *

across to 1 petal before center petal, ch 7, [dc in sl st between petals, ch 7, sc center 2-dc cl of next petal] twice; rep from * to * across, ending last rep at **, ch 7, sc in last ch 4 sp, ch 4, tr in 4th ch of beg ch-8, turn.

ROW 8: Ch 5, dc in first tr, ch 1, dc2tog placing first dc in first ch-4 sp and 2nd dc in next ch-7 sp, *ch 1, (dc, ch 1, dc, picot, ch 1, dc), in same ch-7 sp, ch 1, dc2tog placing first dc in same ch-7 sp and 2nd dc in next ch-7 sp; rep from * across, working 2nd dc of last dc2tog in last ch-4 sp, ch 1, (dc, ch 2, dc) in 4th ch of beg ch-8. Fasten off.

Finishing

Weave in ends wrapping CC twice around MC yarn where it was carried along the side of Stripe 1 for a neater edge. Block.

CHAPTER 2

IT'S A MOD, *Mod World*

The swinging sixties saw the birth of some outrageous fashions (although mainstream now, the miniskirt raised eyebrows at the time). You don't have to don go-go boots to wear these pieces, but you just might want to! Print, pattern, and bold contrasting colors evoke good vibes. Even a plain T-shirt and jeans can be made fabulous with one of these smart accessories.

Finished Size

4¾" wide × 65" long
(12 × 165 cm).

Yarn

DK weight (#3 Light).

Shown here: Berroco Ultra
Alpaca Light (50% super
fine alpaca, 50% Peruvian
wool; 144 yd [132 m]/1¾ oz
[50 g]): #4281 redwood mix
(A), #4209 moonshadow (B),
2 hanks each.

Hook

Sizes G/6 (4 mm). *Adjust hook
size if necessary to obtain correct
gauge.*

Notions

Yarn needle.

Gauge

14 sts = 3" (7.5 cm); 15 rows = 4"
(10 cm).

Op-Art
REVERSIBLE SCARF

Mosaic crochet, which usually involves juggling
multiple balls of yarn, can seem daunting. This
scarf takes away all the complexity by breaking
the pattern down into rows of stripes, so you
only work one color at a time. The best surprise
of the scarf is that the "wrong" side is not
wrong at all but displays another great pattern,
thus giving you two scarves in one.

DESIGNED BY *Robyn Chachula*

Scarf

With A, ch 23.

ROW 1 (RS): Sc in 2nd ch from hook, *sc in next sc, ch 7, sk next 4 ch, sc in next 2 sc; rep from * across, change to B, turn—3 ch-sps.

ROW 2: Ch 1, sc in first sc, *sc in next sc, working in front of ch-7 loops, hdc in next each of 4 ch on foundation ch, sc in next 2 sc; rep from * across, turn.

ROW 3: Ch 1, skipping ch-7 loops, sc in each st across, change to A, turn—22 sc.

ROW 4: Ch 3 (counts as dc here and throughout), *dc in next sc, ch 3, sc in next ch-7 sp, ch 3, sk next 4 sc, dc in next 2 sc; rep from * across, turn—6 ch-3 sps.

ROW 5: Ch 1, sc in first dc, *sc in next dc, ch 7, sk next 2 ch-3 sps, sc in each of next 2 dc; rep from * across, change to B, turn.

ROW 6: Ch 1, sc in first sc, *sc in next sc, working in front of ch-3 sps, tr in each of next 4 sc 3 rows below, sc in each of next 2 sc; rep from * across, turn.

Rep Rows 3–6 until scarf measures 65" (165 cm) or desired length, ending with Row 3 of pattern. Change to A. Fasten off.

EDGING RND: Ch 1, *sc evenly across edge of scarf to corner, 3 sc in corner; rep from * twice, working across top edge, sc in each of next 2 sc, [working over ch-7 loop, sc in each of next 2 sc, sc in each of next 5 sc] twice, working over ch-7 loop, sc in each of next 2 sc, sc in each of next 2 sc, 2 sc in last sc, join with sl st in first sc. Fasten off. Weave in ends.

Finishing

Pin scarf to schematic size with rustproof pins, spray with water and allow to dry.

Inspiration

Bridget Riley is a well-known British artist who came to prominence in the mid-1960s for her distinctive, geometrically intricate paintings known as "op art." The mosaic stitch pattern of this scarf reminds me of Riley's ingenious use of color and shapes.

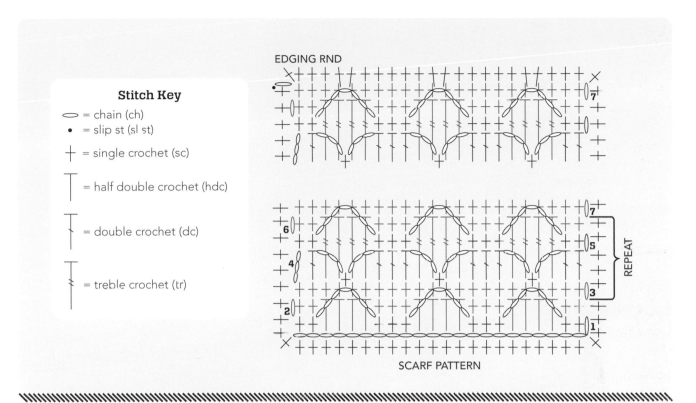

EDGING RND

Stitch Key

◯ = chain (ch)

• = slip st (sl st)

+ = single crochet (sc)

┬ = half double crochet (hdc)

 = double crochet (dc)

 = treble crochet (tr)

REPEAT

SCARF PATTERN

Finished Size

About 8" (20.5 cm) in circumference measured around palm and arm edges, about 7" (18 cm) in circumference around wrist area, and about 11" (28 cm) long. Width measurements are somewhat adjustable—you can overlap the edges more or less than the sample for smaller or larger sizes.

Yarn

DK weight (#3 Light).

Shown here: Blue Sky Alpacas Sport Weight (100% baby alpaca; 110 yd [100 m]/1¾ oz [50 g]): #545 blue spruce (A), 2 skeins; #505 taupe (B), #518 scarlet (C), 1 skein each.

Hook

Size F/5 (3.75 mm). *Adjust hook size if necessary to obtain correct gauge.*

Notions

Stitch markers; yarn needle; sewing pins.

Gauge

20 sts and 20 rows = 4" (10 cm) in pattern (sc blo of the rnd).

Psychedelia
MITTS

These fingerless mittens are crocheted in the round in an unusual way that's reminiscent of an old-fashioned braided rug. The contrasting stripes and fresh colors give these mitts a fun, modern, and slightly psychedelic look.

DESIGNED BY *Brenda K. B. Anderson*

Notes

Mitts are worked in joined rnds with RS facing throughout. The beg of each rnd is the arm end of the mitt—the middle stitch of each rnd is at the finger edge of the mitt. Increases are made at each end of the oval. Shaping for thumb and arm is created by adding more increases than would be necessary to make the oval lay flat.

There are more increases at the finger edge of the oval than at the arm edge.

Carry yarn up the WS of the mitt as you change back and forth between colors.

Left and Right Mitts are made the same—the only difference between them is the way you wrap one edge over the other when you sew the side seam.

Stitch Guide
Single Crochet in Back Loop Only (sc in blo)
This is just like a regular single crochet stitch except you are only working through the back loop of each stitch.

Mitt (make 2)

With A, ch 11.

SET-UP ROW (RS): Working in bottom ridge lp of ch, sc in 2nd ch from hook and each ch across—10 sc.

RND 1 (RS): Rotate work 180 degrees to work across opposite side of foundation ch, insert hook in blo of next st, yo with B and draw through to front, drop A to WS, with B, ch 1, starting in first ch, 2 sc in blo of each of next 2 ch, sc in blo of each of next 6 sc, 2 sc in blo of next 2 sc; rotate work 180 degrees, sk the turning ch, 2 sc in blo of each of next 2 sts, sc in blo of each of next 6 sts, 2 sc in blo of each of next 2 sts, join with sl st in blo of first sc, changing to A on last yo of rnd, drop B to WS—28 sts.

RND 2: With A, ch 1, starting in first st, [2 sc in blo of each of next 2 sts, sc in blo of next 10 sts, 2 sc in blo of each of next 2 sts] twice, join with sl st in blo of first st of rnd to join, changing to B on last yo of rnd, drop A to WS—36 sts.

RND 3: Ch 1, starting in first st, *[sc in blo of next st, 2 sc in blo of next st] twice, sc in blo of next 10 sts, [2 sc in blo of next st, sc in blo of next st] twice; rep from * once, join with sl st in blo of first st of rnd to join, changing to A on last yo of rnd, drop B to WS—44 sts.

RND 4: Ch 1, starting in first st, *[2 sc in blo of next st, sc in blo of next 2 sts] twice, sc in blo of next 10 sts, [sc in blo of next 2 sts, 2 sc in blo of next st] twice; rep from * once, join with sl st in blo of first st of rnd to join, changing to B on last yo of rnd, drop A to WS—52 sts.

RND 5: Ch 1, starting in first st, *[sc in blo of next 3 sts, 2 sc in blo of next st] twice, sc in blo of next 10 sts, [2 sc in blo of next st, sc in blo of next 3 sts] twice; repeat from * once

more, join with sl st in blo of first st of rnd to join, changing to A on last yo of rnd, drop B to WS—60 sts.

RND 6: Ch 1, starting in first st, *[sc in blo of next st, 2 sc in blo of next st, sc in blo of next 3 sts] twice, sc in blo of next 10 sts, [sc in blo of next 3 sts, 2 sc in blo of next st, sc in blo of next st] twice; repeat from * once more, join with sl st in blo of first st of rnd to join, changing to B on last yo of rnd, drop A to WS—68 sts.

RND 7: Ch 1, starting in first st, [sc in blo of next 4 sts, 2 sc in blo of next st, sc in blo of next st] twice, sc in blo of next 10 sts, [sc in blo of next st, 2 sc in blo of next st, sc in blo of next 2 sts] 3 times, [sc in blo of next 2 sts, 2 sc in blo of next st, sc in blo of next st] 3 times, sc in blo of next 10 sts, [sc in blo of next st, 2 sc in blo of next st, sc in blo of next 4 sts] twice, sl st blo of first st of rnd to join, changing to A on last yo of rnd, drop B to WS—78 sts.

of next st, sc in blo of next 6 sts] twice, join with sl st in blo of first st of rnd to join, changing to A on last yo of rnd —96 sts.

RND 10: Ch 1, starting in first st, *[sc in blo of next 5 sts, 2 sc in blo of next st, sc in blo of next 3 sts] twice, sc in blo of next 12 sts, [sc in blo of next 3 sts, 2 sc in blo of next st, sc in blo of next 5 sts] twice; rep from * once more, sl st blo of first st of rnd to join, changing to B on last yo of rnd—104 sts.

RND 11: Ch 1, starting in first st, [sc in blo of next 3 sts, 2 sc in blo of next st, sc in blo of next 5 sts] twice, sc in blo of next 16 sts, [sc in blo of next st, 2 sc in blo of next st, sc in blo of next 4 sts] 3 times, [sc in blo of next 4 sts, 2 sc in blo of next st, sc in blo of next st] 3 times, sc in blo of next 16 sts, [sc in blo of next 5 sts, 2 sc in blo of next st, sc in blo of next 3 sts] twice, sl st blo of first st of rnd to join, changing to A on last yo of rnd, drop B to WS—114 sts.

RND 12: Ch 1, starting in first st, *[sc in blo of next st, 2 sc in blo of next st, sc in blo of next 9 sts] twice, sc in blo of next 13 sts, [sc in blo of next 9 sts, 2 sc in blo of next st, sc in blo of next st] twice; rep from * once more, join with sl st in blo of first st of rnd to join, changing to B on last yo of rnd, drop A to WS—122 sts.

RND 13: Ch 1, starting in first st, [sc in blo of next 6 sts, 2 sc in blo of next st, sc in blo of next 4 sts] twice, sc in blo of next 18 sts, [sc in blo of next 4 sts, 2 sc in blo of next st, sc in blo of next 2 sts] 3 times, [sc in blo of next 2 sts, 2 sc in blo of next st, sc in blo of next 4 sts] 3 times, sc in blo of next 18 sts, [sc in blo of next 4 sts, 2 sc in blo of next st, sc in blo of next 6 sts] twice, join with sl st in blo of first st of rnd to join, changing to A on last yo of rnd, drop B to WS —132 sts.

RND 14: Ch 1, starting in first st, *[sc in blo of next 3 sts, 2 sc in blo of next st, sc in blo of next 9 sts] twice, sc in blo of next 14 sts, [sc in blo of next 9 sts, 2 sc in blo of next st, sc in blo of next 3 sts] twice; rep from * once more, join with sl st in blo of first st of rnd to join, changing to B on last yo of rnd, drop A to WS—140 sts.

RND 8: Ch 1, starting in first st, *[sc in blo of next 3 sts, 2 sc in blo of next st, sc in blo of next 3 sts] twice, sc in blo of next 11 sts, [sc in blo of next 3 sts, 2 sc in blo of next st, sc in blo of next 3 sts] twice; repeat from * once more, join with sl st in blo of first st of rnd to join, changing to B on last yo of rnd, drop A to WS—86 sts.

RND 9: Ch 1, starting in first st, [2 sc in blo of next st, sc in blo of next 6 sts] twice, sc in blo of next 14 sts, [sc in blo of next 3 sts, 2 sc in blo of next st, sc in blo of next st] 3 times, [sc in blo of next st, 2 sc in blo of next st, sc in blo of next 3 sts] 3 times, sc in blo of next 14 sts, [2 sc in blo

RND 15 (THUMBHOLE RND): Ch 1, starting in first st, *[sc in blo of next 8 sts, 2 sc in blo of next st, sc in blo of next 5 sts] twice, sc in blo of next 19 sts, 2 sc in blo of next st, sc in blo of next 13 sts, 2 sc in blo of next st, ch 2, sk each of next 14 sts (for thumb), sc in blo of next st, 2 sc in blo of next st, sc in blo of next 13 sts, 2 sc in blo of next st, sc in blo of next 19 sts, [sc in blo of next 5 sts, 2 sc in blo of next st, sc in blo of next 8 sts] twice, join with sl st in blo of first st of rnd to join, changing to A on last yo of rnd—136 sts. Fasten off B.

RND 16: Ch 1, starting in first st, [sc in blo of next 11 sts, 2 sc in blo of next st, sc in blo of next 44 sts, 2 sc in blo of next st, sc in blo of next 11 sts] twice, join with sl st in blo of first st of rnd to join, changing to C on last yo of rnd—140 sts. Fasten off A.

RND 17: With C, ch 1, starting in first st, [sc in blo of next 6 sts, 2 sc in blo of next st, sc in blo of next 8 sts, 2 sc in blo of next st, sc in blo of next 38 sts, 2 sc in blo of next st, sc in blo of next 8 sts, 2 sc in blo of next st, sc in blo of next 6 sts] twice, join with sl st in blo of first st of rnd to join, do not change color—148 sts.

RND 18: Ch 1, starting in first st, [sc in blo of next 15 sts, 2 sc in blo of next st, sc in blo of next 42 sts, 2 sc in blo of next st, sc in blo of next 15 sts] twice, join with sl st in blo of first st of rnd to join, do not change color—152 sts.

RND 19: Ch 1, starting in first st, [sc in blo of next 10 sts, 2 sc in blo of next st, sc in blo of next 7 sts, 2 sc in blo of next st, sc in blo of next 38 sts, 2 sc in blo of next st, sc in blo of next 7 sts, 2 sc in blo of next st, sc in blo of next 10 sts] twice, join with sl st in blo of first st of rnd to join, changing to A on last yo of rnd—160 sts.

RND 20: With A, ch 1, starting in first st, sc in blo of each st around—160 sts.

Note: *Work the sl sts in the next rnd loosely enough so that the edge doesn't pucker, but tightly enough so that the edge will not stretch out.*

RND 21: Sl st in each st around; place removable stitch marker in 24th, 60th, 101st, and 137th sts—160 sts.

Fasten off. Weave in ends.

Thumb

RND 1: With RS facing, join B with sl st in any st of thumb opening, ch 1, sc in blo of each st around, join with sl st in blo of first st of rnd, changing to A on last yo of rnd, drop B to WS—16 sts.

RND 2: Ch 1, starting in first st, sc in each st around—16 sts.

Note: *Work the sl sts in the next rnd loosely enough so that the edge doesn't pucker, but tightly enough so that the edge will not stretch out.*

RND 3: Sl st in each st around.

Fasten off. Weave in ends.

Finishing

Matching stitch markers, pin top and bottom of side seams together. Make sure mitts overlap in opposite ways from each other (the overlaps should mirror each other). The sl st rnd (the very edge of overlap) should match up with the 3rd A ring in from the C stripe. Pin side edge in place. Check fit of mitt. Adjust amount of overlap if necessary. Using yarn needle and A, sew side seams on RS of mitt just to the inside of the slip stitch rnd. Turn mitt inside out and using A and yarn needle, carefully stitch the underlapping layer in place. Be especially careful not to let your stitches show on the RS of mitt. Weave in ends. Turn RS out. Spray block lightly if necessary.

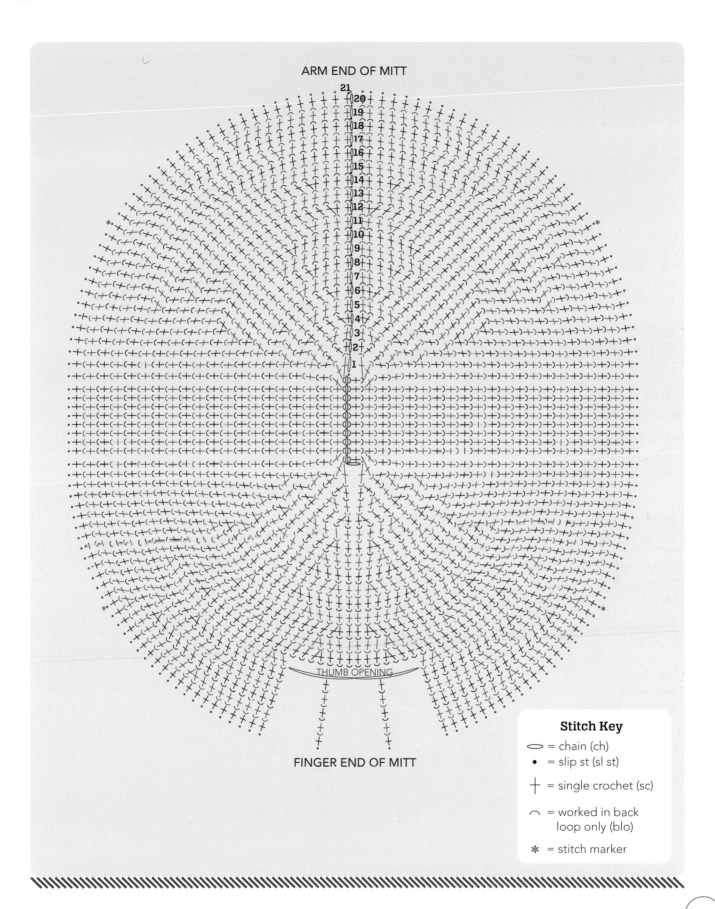

FINGER END OF MITT

THUMB OPENING

Stitch Key

◯ = chain (ch)

• = slip st (sl st)

+ = single crochet (sc)

⌒ = worked in back loop only (blo)

* = stitch marker

Finished Size

About 11" wide × 8" tall × 2½" deep (28 × 20.5 × 6.5 cm).

Yarn

DK weight (#3 Light).

Shown here: Cascade Yarns Cascade 220 Sport (100% Peruvian highland wool; 164 yd [150 m]/1¾ oz [50 g]): #7827 goldenrod (A), 2 hanks; #8010 natural (B), #4002 jet (C), #8906 blue topaz (D), #8895 Christmas red (F), 1 hank each.

Hook

Size G/7 (4.5 mm). *Adjust hook size if necessary to obtain correct gauge.*

Notions

Yarn needle; large magnetic snap; two 1½" (3.8 cm) diameter silver D rings; 44" (112 cm) shoulder strap; 3" (7.5 cm) by 4" (10 cm) needle-felting brush mat; pen-style needle felting tool.

Gauge

20 sts (measured from point to point of chevron) and 5 rows = 4" (10 cm) in zigzag chevron stitch pattern before felting; 20 sts (measured from point to point of chevron) and 5 rows = 2¾" (7 cm) in zigzag chevron stitch pattern after felting; flower motif = 5" (12.5 cm) in diameter.

Note

If substituting yarns, make sure to felt a swatch to see how small your finished project will measure. Unfelted size of purse was about 14" (35.5 cm) wide, by 10" (25.5 cm) tall, by 3" (7.5 cm) wide.

Petula PURSE

This purse is an introduction to a great technique—felting. Felting a project after crocheting may feel like a time-consuming extra step, but it actually gives you a fantastic canvas to work on. Felting makes the purse completely useable without having to sew in a lining, and felted fabric creates a great background for embroidery or needle felting (as with the flower attached here). An added bonus is that if you're at all messy in seaming or stitching, all is hidden when felted!

DESIGNED BY *Robyn Chachula*

Stitch Guide

Picot: Ch 4, sl st last sc made.

Back

With A, ch 63.

ROW 1 (RS): 2 dc in 4th ch from hook (sk ch sts count as dc), *dc in next 6 ch, [dc3tog over next 3 ch] twice, dc in next 6 ch**, 3 dc in each of next 2 ch; rep from * across, ending last rep at **, 3 dc in last ch, turn—60 dc.

ROWS 2–4: Ch 3 (count as dc here and throughout), 2 dc in first dc, *dc in next 6 dc, [dc3tog over next 3 dc] twice, dc in next 6 dc**, 3 dc in next 2 dc; rep from * across, ending last rep at **, 3 dc in last st, turn. At end of last row, change to B.

ROW 5: With B, rep Row 2, turn, change to C.

ROW 6: With C, ch 1, 2 sc in first dc, *sc in next 7 dc, [sc2tog over next 2 dc] twice, sc in next 7 dc**, 2 sc in each of next 2 dc; rep from * across, ending last rep at **, 2 sc in last st, turn, change to A.

ROW 7: With A, ch 3 (counts as dc throughout), 2 dc in first sc, *dc in next 6 sc**, [dc3tog over next 3 sc] twice, dc in next 6 sc, 3 dc in next 2 sc; rep from * across, ending last rep at **, 3 dc in last sc, turn.

ROWS 8–18: Rep Rows 2–7; then rep Rows 2–6, turn.

ROW 19: Ch 3, *dc in each of next 6 sc, [dc3tog over next 3 sc] twice, dc in each of next 6 sc**, 3 dc in each of next 2 sc; rep from * across, ending last rep at **, dc in last st, turn—56 sts.

ROW 20: Ch 3, dc in each of next 4 sts, *[dc3tog over next 3 dc] twice**, dc in next 6 dc, 3 dc in each of next 2 dc, dc in next 6 dc; rep from * across, ending last rep at **, dc in each of last 5 sts, turn—52 sts.

ROW 21: Ch 3, dc in each of next 2 sts, *[dc3tog over next 3 dc] twice**, dc in next 6 dc, 3 dc in each of next 2 dc, dc in next 6 dc; rep from * across, ending last rep at **, dc in each of last 3 sts, turn—48 sts.

ROW 22: Ch 3, *[dc3tog over next 3 dc] twice**, dc in next 6 dc, 3 dc in each of next 2 dc, dc in next 6 dc; rep from * across, ending last rep at **, dc in last st, turn—44 sts.

Inspiration

Petula Clark is an English singer and composer who began her career on BBC Radio singing for the troops during WWII. She had hits with such songs as *Downtown* and *Don't Sleep in the Subway*. This purse is so named for the many album covers and publicity stills that feature Petula either holding a colorful bloom or amidst a field of flowers.

Back/Flap Curved End

ROW 23A (RS): Ch 2, sk first dc, dc3tog over next 3 dc, hdc in next dc, sc in each of next 2 dc, sl st in each of next 3 dc—7 sts. Fasten off.

ROW 23B: With RS facing, sk next 2 dc after Row 23a, join B with sl st in next dc, ch 2, sk first st, dc in each of next 6 dc, [dc3tog over next 3 dc] twice, dc in each of next 5 dc, dc2tog over next 2 dc, turn, change to C—14 dc.

ROW 24: With C, ch 1, sc3tog over first 3 sts, sc in next st, [sc3tog over next 3 sts] twice, sc in next st, sc3tog over next 3 sts, change to A, turn—6 sc.

ROW 25: Ch 2, sk first st, dc4tog over next 4 sts, ch 2, sl st in last sts. Fasten off.

ROW 23C: With RS facing, sk next 2 dc after Row 23b, join A with sl st in next dc, sl st to each of next 2 dc, sc in each of next 2 dc, hdc in next dc, dc3tog over next 3 dc, ch 1, sl st to top of tch. Fasten off.

Back Bottom Curved End

ROW 1: With WS facing, working over opposite side of foundation ch, sk 10 ch sts, join C with sl st in next ch, ch 1, sc2tog in first 2 ch, sc in each of next 6 ch, [sc2tog over next 2 ch] twice, sc in each of next 7 ch, 2 sc in each of next 2 ch, sc in each of next 7 ch, [sc2tog over next 2 ch] twice, sc in each of next 6 ch, sc2tog over next 2 ch, turn, leaving rem sts unworked, change to B—36 sc.

ROW 2: Ch 2 (does not count as a st), sk first sc, dc in next 4 sc, [dc3tog over next 3 sc] twice, dc in each of next 6 sc, 3 dc in each of next 2 sc, dc in each of next 6 sc, [dc3tog over next 3 sc] twice, dc in each of next 3 sc, dc2tog over last 2 sc, change to A, turn—30 dc.

ROW 3: Ch 2 (does not count as a st), sk first dc, dc in next dc, [dc3tog over next 3 dc] twice, hdc in each of next 2 dc, sc in each of next 3 dc, sl st in each of next 4 dc, sc in each of next 3 dc, hdc in each of next 2 dc, [dc3tog over next 3 dc] twice, dc2tog over last 2 sts, turn—20 sts.

ROW 4: Ch 2 (does not count as a st), sk first dc, dc2tog over next 2 sts, sk next 2 sc, sl st in each of next 10 sts, sk next 2 sts, dc2tog over next 2 sts, ch 2, sl st to last st. Fasten off.

Front

Work same as for Back through Row 10, change to B.

First Top Flat End Section

ROW 1A: Ch 2 (does not count as a st), sk first dc, dc2tog over next 2 dc, dc in each of next 4 dc, [dc3tog over next 3 dc] twice, dc in each of next 4 dc, dc3tog over next 3 dc, turn, leaving rem sts unworked, change to C—12 dc.

ROW 2A: With C, ch 1, sc2tog over first 2 dc, sc in each of next 2 dc, [sc2tog over next 2 dc] twice, sc in each of next 2 dc, sc2tog over last 2 dc, turn, change to A—8 sc.

ROW 3A: With B, ch 2, sk first sc, dc6tog over next 6 sc, ch 2, sl st to last sc. Fasten off.

Second and Third Top Flat End Sections

Join yarn with sl st in next dc after Row 1a of last section, rep Rows 1a–3a.

Bottom Curved End

Work same as Back Bottom Curved End.

First Side

With A, make an adjustable ring (see Glossary).

ROW 1 (RS): Ch 3 (counts as dc here and throughout), 7 dc in ring, turn, pull ring closed.

ROW 2: Ch 3, 2 dc in first dc, dc in each of next 2 dc, 3 dc in each of next 2 dc, dc in each of next 2 dc, 3 dc in last dc, turn—16 dc.

ROWS 3–4: Ch 2, sk first st, dc2tog over next 2 sts, dc in each of next 4 sts, 3 dc in each of next 2 sts, dc in each of next 4 sts, dc3tog over last 3 sts, turn. At end of last row, change to B.

ROW 5: Rep Row 3, change to C.

ROW 6: Ch 1, sc2tog over first 2 dc, sc in each of next 5 dc, 2 sc in each of next 2 dc, sc in each of next 5 dc, sc2tog over last 2 sts, turn, change to A.

ROWS 7–8: Rep Row 3.

ROWS 9–21: Rep Rows 3–8 (twice); rep Row 3.

Second Side

Work same as First Side through Row 20.

ROW 21: Ch 2, sk first st, dc2tog over next 2 sts, dc in each of next 4 sts, 3 dc in next dc, sl st in space between center 2 sts in last row of First Side, dc in each of next 4 sts, dc3tog over last 3 sts, turn. Fasten off.

Side Panel Filler Motif

ROW 1: With RS facing, join B with sl st in first st on last row of First Side, ch 2, sk first st, dc2tog over next 2 dc, dc in next 2 dc, dc3tog over next 3 dc on First Side, dc3tog over next 3 dc on Second Side, dc in each of next 2 dc, dc3tog over last 3 dc, turn, change to C—8 sts.

ROW 2: Ch 1, sc2tog over first 2 sts, [sc2tog over next 2 sts] 3 times, turn, change to A—4 sts.

ROW 3: Ch 2, dc4tog over all 4 sts, ch 2, sl st to last st holding last leg of dc4tog. Fasten off.

Rep Side Panel Filler Motif on opposite side of Sides.

Finishing

Sl st embroider (see Glossary) to add stripes to fabric. With C, sl st across all C rows on back, front, and side panels. With D, sl st across top of each of the following rows: Back Rows 1, 7, 13, 19; Front Rows 1 and 7; Side Rows 1, 7, 13, 19. With RS facing, pin assembled Side Panel to Front and Back panels. Whipstitch (see Glossary) Side Panel to Front and Back to form purse. With RS facing, join A with sl st to top of Side Panel, ch 1, sc evenly around purse opening including flap, join with sl st in first sc. Fasten off. Weave in ends. Felt purse to size by hand. Immerse purse in hot water and massage, and then submerge in cold water and massage. Rep until stitch definition is nearly invisible. Attach magnetic snap to bottom of flap and opposite front. Pinch side panel in half and sew closed to form pucker. Sew D ring to each side of purse with A. Attach shoulder strap to rings.

Flower Motif

With E, make an adjustable ring.

RND 1 (RS): Ch 1, *sc in ring, picot; rep from * 7 times, join with sl st in first sc—8 sc; 8 picots.

RND 2: (Sc, hdc, 3 dc, hdc, sc) in each ch-4 sp around, join with sl st in first sc—8 petals.

RND 3: Ch 1, sc between first and last sc of Rnd 2, *ch 5, sk next petal**, sc between next 2 sc; rep from * around, ending last rep at **, join with sl st in first sc—8 ch-5 sps.

RND 4: (Sc, hdc, 4 dc, hdc, sc) in each ch-5 sp around, join with sl st in first sc—8 petals.

RND 5: Ch 1, sc between first and last sc of Rnd 4, *ch 7, sk next petal**, sc bet next 2 sc; rep from * around, ending last rep at **, join with sl st in first sc—8 ch-7 sps.

RND 6: 10 Sc in each ch-7 sp around, join with sl st in first sc.

RND 7: Ch 1, sc between first and last sc of Rnd 6, *ch 8, sk next 10 sc**, sc in sp before next sc; rep from * around, ending last rep at **, join with sl st in first sc.

RND 8: 12 sc in each ch-8 sp around, join with sl st in first sc. Fasten off.

Using photo as a guide, needle felt center to flap by placing flap on needle brush mat; insert needle pen over and over the center and Rnd 1 of Flower until stitch definition is nearly invisible. Needle felt last rnd entirely. Needle felt each sc in Rnds 3, 5, and 7.

Stitch Key

- ⬭ = chain (ch)
- • = slip st (sl st)
- † = single crochet (sc)
- ⌠ = long single crochet (long sc)
- | = half double crochet (hdc)
- ⊥ = double crochet (dc)
- ⋏ = single crochet 2 together (sc2tog)
- ⋏ = double crochet 2 together (dc2tog)
- ⋏ = double crochet 3 together (dc3tog)
- ⋏ = double crochet 4 together (dc4tog)
- ⋏ = double crochet 6 together (dc6tog)
- ◊ = picot
- ◯ = adjustable ring
- ● = sl st embroidery in jet (C)
- ● = sl st embroidery in blue topaz (D)

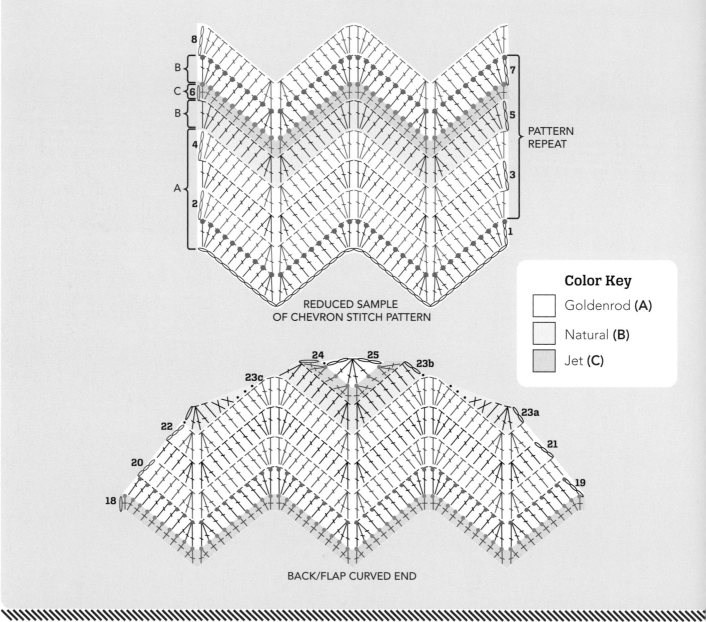

REDUCED SAMPLE
OF CHEVRON STITCH PATTERN

PATTERN REPEAT

Color Key

- ☐ Goldenrod (A)
- ☐ Natural (B)
- ▨ Jet (C)

BACK/FLAP CURVED END

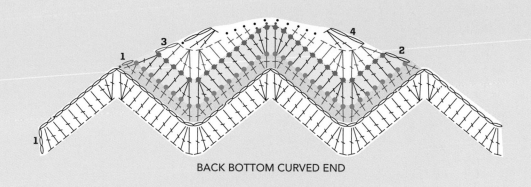

BACK BOTTOM CURVED END

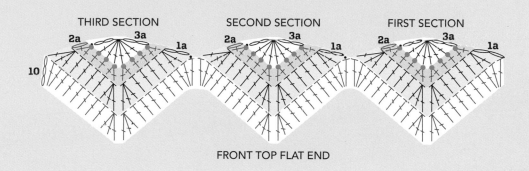

THIRD SECTION SECOND SECTION FIRST SECTION

FRONT TOP FLAT END

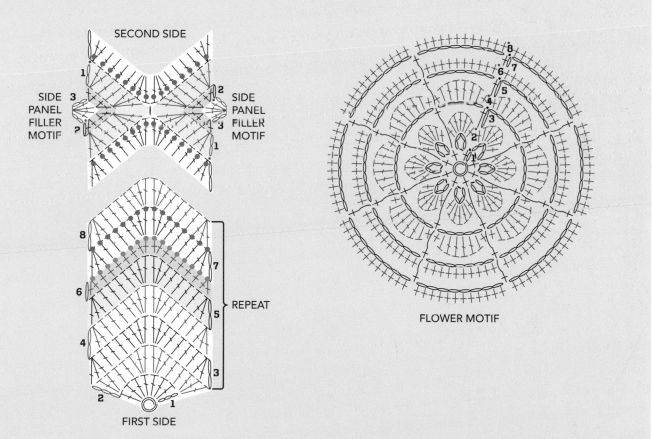

SECOND SIDE

SIDE PANEL FILLER MOTIF

SIDE PANEL FILLER MOTIF

REPEAT

FIRST SIDE

FLOWER MOTIF

Roundel SCARF

Finished Size

7¾" wide (including marble fringe) by 73" long from end to end (19.5 × 185.5 cm).

Yarn

DK weight (#3 Light).

Shown here: Manos del Uruguay Silk Blend (30% silk, 70% merino extrafine wool; 150 yd [135 m]/1¾ oz [50 g]): #300X topaz (A), 2 skeins; #3043 juniper (B), #3059 kohl (C), 1 skein each. Yarn distributed by Fairmount Fibers.

Hooks

Sizes E/4 (3.50 mm) and F/5 (3.75 mm). *Adjust hook sizes if necessary to obtain correct gauge.*

Notions

Yarn needle; rustproof pins.

Gauge

After blocking, with larger hook, Large Marble = 2⅝" (6.7 cm) in diameter; Medium Marble = 2¼" (5.5 cm) in diameter; and Small Marble = 1⅜" (3.5 cm) in diameter.

The roundel is a circular symbol seen in many settings, such as the symbol for the London Underground and the logo of the British Royal Air Force. Mods customized this symbol for use in fashions of the era. This scarf, which can also be worn as a belt, updates the classic symbol with contrasting jewel tones.

DESIGNED BY *Shelby Allaho*

Small Marble

(make 14 in B, 11 in C)

RND 1: With larger hook, make an adjustable ring, insert
hook in ring, yo and pull up a lp, ch 4, 15 tr in ring—16 dc.
Invisible fasten off (see Stitch Guide). Pull on tail end of
yarn to close ring.

Medium Marble (make 12 in C)

RND 1: Work Rnd 1 of Small Marble. Do not fasten off.

RND 2: Ch 3 (counts as dc), dc in first st, 2 dc in each st
around—32 dc. Invisible fasten off.

Large Marble (make 11 in B)

RND 1: Work Rnd 1 of Small Marble. Do not fasten off.

RND 2: Ch 4 (counts as tr), tr in first st, 2 tr in each st
around—32 tr. Invisible fasten off.

To embellish the center of each Large Marble using A and
a yarn needle, bring the needle up in the center of the
Marble, and then go down in each of the sts in Rnd 1.

Joining Center Panel Marbles

Note: *When joining a Marble, work the st in the Large
Marble and the horizontal lp below the front lp on
the edge of the Medium Marble, or Small Marble,
simultaneously.*

**Using size E/4 (3.50 mm) hook and A, wrap yarn twice
around hook and pick up a Large Marble. Working into
the stitches made in Rnd 2, (hdc, ch 1) in each of first
14 sts, *join a Medium Marble to the Large Marble as
follows: Place the Marbles back to back, then [hdc, ch 1],
in each of next 2 sts in the Large Marble and in any 2
adjacent sts on the Medium Marble*, (hdc, ch 1) in each
of next 14 sts on the Large Marble**, rep from * to * in
last 2 sts. Invisible fasten off.

Rep from ** to ** once. Join this Large Marble to the last
set of previously joined Marbles. Place this Marble back to
back with a previously joined Medium Marble, and then
(hdc, ch 1) in each of the last 2 sts in the Large Marble and
the 15th and 16th sts from where the Medium Marble was
joined to its Large Marble. Invisible fasten off. Repeat this
sequence 7 more times—9 Large Marbles and 10 Medium
Marbles joined in a strip.

Joining of Scarf Ends

Note: *One Large Marble will be joined to one Small
Marble, one Medium Marble, one Small Marble, and to
one Medium Marble at one end of Center Panel.*

Using size E/4 (3.50 mm) hook and A, wrap yarn twice
around the hook and pick up a Large Marble, working
into the stitches made in Rnd 2, (hdc, ch 1) in each of the
first 12 sts, *pick up one Small Marble in color B, place
Marbles back to back, and then work (hdc, ch 1) in each
of next 2 sts on Large Marble and in any 2 adjacent sts
on Small Marble*. **Pick up one Medium Marble, place
the Large and Medium Marbles back to back, work (hdc,
ch 1) in each of next 2 sts on Large Marble and in any 2
adjacent sts on Medium Marble**; rep from * to * once,
(hdc, ch 1) in each of next 12 sts on Large Marble, join

this group of Marbles to Medium Marble at one end of Center Panel as follows: (Hdc, ch 1) in each of last 2 sts on Large Marble and in the 15th and 16th sts from where the Medium Marble was joined onto the Large Marble in the Center Panel. Invisible fasten off. Rep these instructions for the other end of scarf.

Bottom Edging

With larger hook and A, ch 299.

ROW 1: Sc in 6th ch from hook, *ch 7, sk next 3 ch, tr5tog over next 5 ch, ch 7, sk next 3 ch, sc in next ch, ch 3, sk 1 ch, sc in next ch; rep from * across, turn—21 tr5tog clusters.

ROW 2: Ch 1, sc in next ch-3 sp, *ch 7, sc in next ch-7 sp, ch 5, sc in next ch-7 sp, ch 7, sc in next ch-3 sp; rep from * across, turn—21 ch-5 sps; 42 ch-7 sps.

ROW 3: 7 sc in first ch-7 sp, *in next ch 3 sp, work (2 sc, then join a Small Marble [beg with a Marble in yarn C, then alternate between Marbles in yarns B and C] by inserting the hook in the ch-5 sp, and then in the center hole of the back side of a Small Marble, yo, and draw up a lp that is large enough for the Small Marble to just meet the edge of the ch-5 sp, yo and draw through both lps on hook, 2 sc)**, 7 sc in each of next 2 ch-7 sps; rep from * once; rep from * to ** once, 7 sc in next ch-7 sp, rotate work to work across bottom edge.

Note: In next row, the Edging will be joined to the Center Panel of Marbles.

ROW 4: Working across foundation ch at base of Row 1, 2 sc in ch-1 sp of Row 1, ch 6, sc in nearest st that joins the Small Marble to the Large Marble at the end of the scarf, sc in each of first 2 ch of ch-6, hdc in each of next 2 ch, and dc in each of last 2 ch, sc in same ch 1 sp in base of Row 1, 3 sc in next ch-3 sp. Continue to work the instruction sequences on page 66 in the following order: Sequence 2, Sequence 1, Sequence 3, [work the full instructions for Sequence 1, Sequence 2, Sequence 1, Sequence 3] 9 times; then work Sequence 1, Sequence 2, Sequence 1 from * to *, 2 sc in same sp. Invisible fasten off in first sc in Row 3.

Sequence 1—
Edging to Center Panel Bridge

3 sc in next ch-3 sp, sc in foll ch-1 sp, ch 6, sc in nearest st that joins the Medium Marble to the Large Marble, sc in each of first 2 ch of ch-6, hdc in each of next 2 ch, and dc in each of last 2 ch, sc in same ch-1 sp in base of Row 1, 3 sc in next ch-3 sp.

Sequence 2—
Edging to Large Marble Join

Sc in next 2 ch (at base of first 2 tr) and then join the edging to the Large Marble in the following manner: Insert hook in next ch and then into the horizontal lp underneath the front lp of the 7th st from where it was joined to the last Marble, *yo, and draw through work, yo and draw through 2 lps on hook*, insert hook in same ch in edging, and then in next horizontal lp in the Large Marble; rep from * to * once, sc in next 2 ch (at base of 2 tr).

Sequence 3—
Edging to Medium Marble Join

Sc in next ch (at base of first tr) and then join the edging to the Medium Marble in the following manner: *Insert hook in next ch and then in the horizontal lp under the 6th st from where the Medium Marble is joined to the Large Marble, yo and draw through work, yo and draw through 2 lps on hook; rep from * twice, working in next 2 ch on foundation ch and in next 2 dc of Medium Marble, sc in last tr.

Top Edging

Work same as Bottom Edging, except do not attach any Small Marbles in Row 3.

Replace the instructions for joining the Small Marble with a sc (in other words, work 5 sc in each ch-5 sp).

End Edging

Note: The sts worked in the Marbles are to be worked in the horizontal lps that are below the front lps of the edge sts.

ROW 1: With WS of work facing, begin on one end of scarf. With RS facing, join A in sc at the base of the last bridge, ch 17, *join next Small and Medium Marbles together by making a sl st in 3rd st of each Marble from where they are joined to the scarf*, ch 15, sk next sl st in Medium Marble in the 9th sl st from last sl st, ch 14, sk next 6 sts, sl st in next dc, ch 15; rep from * to * once, ch 17, sl st in sc at the base of the last bridge on this side, turn.

ROW 2: 20 hdc in first ch-17 sp, 18 hdc in next ch-15 sp, 17 hdc in next ch-14 sp, 18 hdc in next ch-15 sp, 20 hdc in next ch-17 sp. Sl st back in sc at the base of the last bridge on this side. Fasten off. Rep End Edging on the other end of Scarf.

Finishing

Weave in ends. Pin on a blocking board. Wet or steam block.

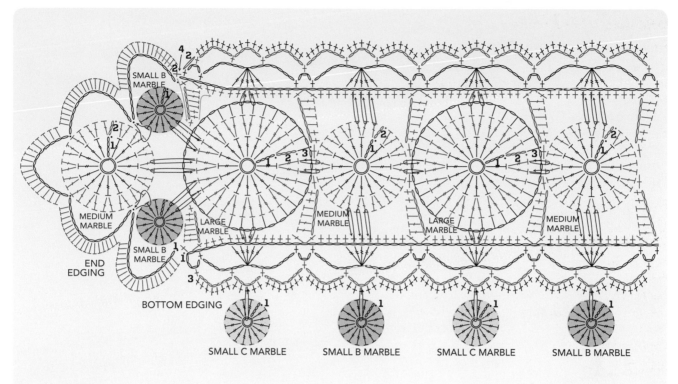

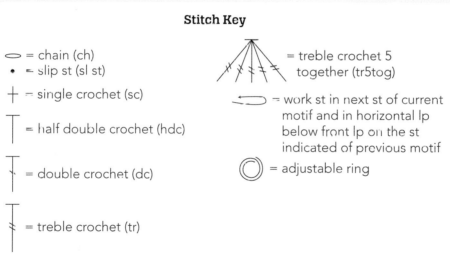

SMALL C MARBLE   SMALL B MARBLE   SMALL C MARBLE   SMALL B MARBLE

Stitch Key

◯ = chain (ch)

• = slip st (sl st)

+ = single crochet (sc)

T = half double crochet (hdc)

↑ = double crochet (dc)

‡ = treble crochet (tr)

⋀ = treble crochet 5 together (tr5tog)

↩ = work st in next st of current motif and in horizontal lp below front lp on the st indicated of previous motif

◎ = adjustable ring

Finished Size

6" wide × 9½" long (15 × 24 cm).

Yarn

Sportweight (#2 Fine).

Shown here: Filatura di Crosa Zarina (100% merino superwash; 180 yd [165 m]/1¾ oz [50 g]): #1404 black (A), 2 skeins; #1944 fawn heather (B), #1396 off-white (C), 1 skein each. Yarn distributed by Tahki-Stacy Charles, Inc.

Hook

Size D/3 (3.25 mm). *Adjust hook size if necessary to obtain correct gauge.*

Notions

Magnetic button, snap, or clasp; yarn needle; fabric stiffener.

Gauge

28 sts and 34 rows = 4" (10 cm) in sc or TC.

Notes

The body of the clutch is worked in single crochet.

Flap is worked in tapestry crochet (TC), following a chart for color changes.

Side seams are sewn together. Edging in reverse crochet is made around the cover and base chain (of the body of the clutch). Button is sewn on last.

Edie CLUTCH

Leopard print is such a classic. It adds a lot of interest to an otherwise basic outfit when used in small accessories like belts, shoes, and clutches. With just a small section of tapestry crochet, this exciting piece will ease you into this otherwise intimidating technique.

DESIGNED BY *Linda Skuja*

Stitch Guide

Tapestry Crochet (TC): Worked with 2 colors, work in sc with first color, carrying 2nd color on top of sts in row below and working over carried color with first color.

Changing Color: Work last sc of first color until 2 loops are on hook, yo with 2nd color and draw through 2 loops on hook, drop first color and carry on top of previous row; continue with 2nd color, working over first color.

Clutch

Front

With A, ch 67.

ROW 1: Sc in 2nd ch from hook and in each ch across, turn—66 sc.

ROWS 2–43: Ch 1, sc in each sc across, turn.

Bottom

ROW 44: Ch 1, sc blo of each st across, turn.

ROW 45: Ch 1, sc in each sc across, turn.

Back

ROW 1: Ch 1, sc blo of each st across, turn.

ROWS 2–50: Ch 1, sc in each sc across, turn. Complete last st with B, fasten off A.

Flap

ROW 1: With B, ch 1, sc in blo of each sc across, turn.

ROW 2: Ch 1, sc2tog (see Glossary) over next 2 sc, sc in each of next 62 sc, sc2tog over last 2 sc, turn—64 sts.

Attach C and work in TC for flap.

Inspiration

Edith Minturn "Edie" Sedgwick was an American actress, socialite, fashion model, heiress, and "it girl" of her generation. Her name and style came back into notice when the 2006 movie *Factory Girl*, which documented her rise and fall, was released. While Sedgwick always wore bold graphic prints typical of the 1960s, many images of her feature an outlandish leopard print coat with a lavish portrait collar. I'd like to think Edie would approve of this crochet homage.

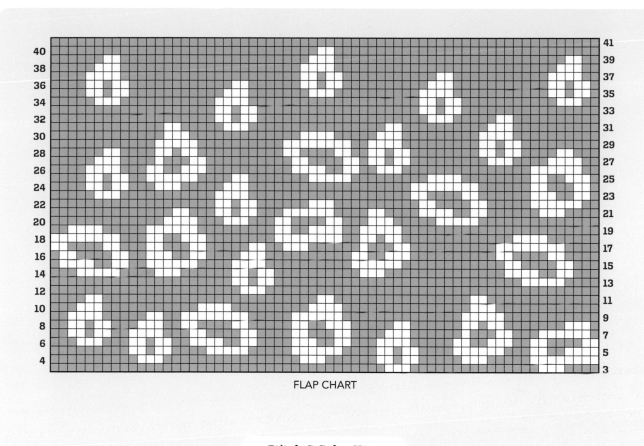

FLAP CHART

Stitch & Color Key
- ☐ (gray) sc in Fawn Heather **(B)**
- ☐ sc in Off-white **(C)**

ROW 3: Ch 1, working TC with B, sc in each of next 4 sts, 4 fawn heather, with C, sc in each of next 3 sts; with B, sc in each of next 15 sts, 4 fawn heather; with C, sc in each of next 3 sts; with B, sc in each of next 39 sts, turn. First row of Chart complete.

Continue working in TC following Chart for color changes. Fasten off.

Finishing

With WS facing, sew side seams.

Edging

With RS facing, join A with sl st in top right-hand corner of Flap, ch 1; working from left to right, rev sc (see Glossary) evenly across side bottom and other side edge of Flap; working in opposite side of foundation ch on top edge of Front, rev sc in each st across, join with sl st in first rev sc. Weave in ends. Block and stiffen the clutch. With RS facing, center button or snap on Front and sew on; sew on button or snap in corresponding position on Flap.

Finished Size

4½" wide × 62" long before joining (11.5 × 157.5 cm).

Yarn

Sportweight (#2 Fine).

Shown here: Zitron Unisono #1170 (100% virgin wool; 328 yd [300 m]/3½ oz [100 g]): #1170 solid off-white (MC), #1210 red, green, aqua multicolored (CC), 1 skein each. Yarn distributed by Skacel.

Hook

Size F/5 (3.75 mm). *Adjust hook size if necessary to obtain correct gauge.*

Notions

Yarn needle.

Gauge

One chevron = 2¼" (5.5 cm) wide; 6 rows = 2" (5 cm), after blocking.

Note

Gauge is crucial to the success of this project. The self-striping yarn lines up perfectly in the stitch pattern and gauge after blocking. Take care to block your swatch. It may be necessary to rip back and crochet more or less loosely.

Rocksteady
COWL

This cowl may look like it has a million ends to weave in, but the yarn does all the work! This self-striping sock yarn matches up perfectly with a neutral color, and the chevrons in the stitch pattern make a bold and graphic, yet cozy, statement. Wear it doubled for extra warmth during chilly winter days.

DESIGNED BY *Sharon Zientara*

Stitch Guide

Color Change: Work st indicated to last yo, complete last yo with new color. Before making next st, move old color of yarn between hook and new yarn and complete next st. Lightly tug on the old yarn to ensure a clean color change.

Cowl

With MC, ch 29.

ROW 1: Working in bottom ridge lps of foundation ch, dc in 4th ch from hook (beg ch-3 counts as dc), [sk next ch, dc in next ch] twice, dc in next ch, 5 dc in next ch, dc in each of next 2 ch, [sk next ch, dc in next ch] twice, change to CC (see Stitch Guide) in last yo of last dc, with CC, [sk next ch, dc in next ch] twice, dc in next ch, 5 dc in next ch, dc in each of next 2 ch, [sk next ch, dc in next ch] twice, dc in last ch, turn.

ROW 2: With CC, ch 1 (does not count as st), sc in first 13 dc, change to MC, sc in each st across, turn.

ROW 3: Ch 3 (counts as dc here and throughout), dc in next sc, *[sk next sc, dc in next sc] twice, dc in next sc, 5 dc in next sc, dc in each of next 2 sc, [sk next sc, dc in next sc] twice, change to CC, with CC, [sk next sc, dc in next sc] twice, dc in next sc, 5 dc in next sc, dc in next 2 sc, [sk next sc, dc in next sc] twice, dc in last sc, turn.

ROWS 4–5: Rep Rows 2–3 once.

ROW 6: Ch 1, sc in each st across without changing color, turn.

ROW 7: Working with CC, change to MC, rep Row 3.

ROWS 8–11: Maintaining established color sequence, rep Rows 2–3 (twice).

ROW 12: With MC, rep Row 6.

ROW 13: Rep Row 3.

ROWS 14–180: Rep Rows 2–13 (13 times); rep Rows 2–12 once.

Finishing

Weave in ends. Wet block to measurements. Sl st seam (see Glossary) ends of cowl together.

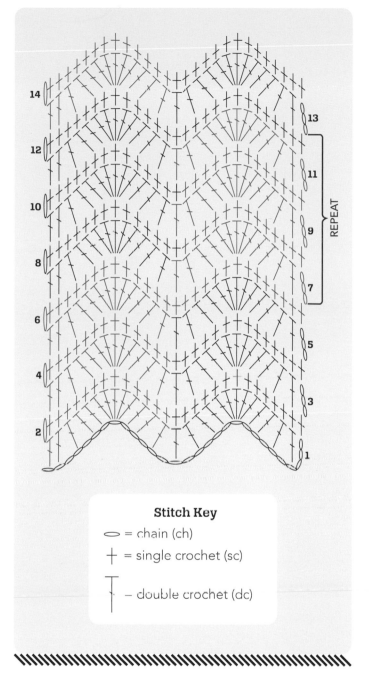

14
13
12
11
10
9
8
7
6
5
4
3
2
1

REPEAT

Stitch Key

◯ = chain (ch)

+ = single crochet (sc)

⊤ = double crochet (dc)

Inspiration

In the 1960s, Jamaican street culture informed the style of mod-era fashion, especially in the United Kingdom. With Jamaican culture came all forms of music, including rocksteady, which was popular after ska and before reggae. The graphic rainbow shades in this scarf paired with the clean lines of a chevron stitch remind me of the colorful nature of Jamaican culture with a touch of British sophistication.

Beatnik CAP

Finished Size

Cap measures 21½" (54.5 cm) in circumference.

Yarn

Sportweight (#2 Fine).

Shown here: Valley Yarns Northampton Sport (100% wool; 164 yd [150 m]/1¾ oz [50 g]): light gray, 3 hanks. Yarn distributed by WEBS.

Hook

Size D/3 (3.25 mm). *Adjust hook size if necessary to obtain correct gauge.*

Gauge

First 3 rnds = 2½" (6.5 cm) in diameter. 22 sts and 16 rows in sc = 4" (10 cm).

This brimmed beret calls to mind a girl reading Kerouac in a smoky lounge or coffeehouse. I envision her waiting for a poetry reading to start and wearing an amazing pair of boots and a sleek black turtleneck. Today, this cap seems more playful than brooding. Add a second color in either the brim or the puff-stitch rounds to give it a touch of whimsy.

DESIGNED BY *Yoko Hatta*

Stitch Guide

Beginning Puff St (beg puff st): Ch 3, [yo, insert hook in next st or sp, yo, draw yarn through and up to level of work] 3 times in same st or sp, yo, draw yarn through 7 loops on hook.

Puff St: [Yo, insert hook in next st or sp, yo, draw yarn though and up to level of work] 4 times in same st or sp, yo, draw yarn through 9 loops on hook.

Beginning Shell (sh): (Beg puff st, ch 2, puff st) in same st or sp.

Shell (sh): (Puff st, ch 2, puff st) in same st or sp.

Beginning Increase Shell (beg inc sh): (Puff st, ch 2, puff st, ch 2, puff st) in same st or sp.

Increase Shell (inc sh): (Puff st, ch 2, puff st, ch 2, puff st) in same st or sp.

Crown

Ch 5, join with sl st in first ch to form a ring.

RND 1: Ch 3 (counts as dc here and throughout), 11 dc in ring, join with sl st in top of beg ch-3—12 dc.

RND 2: Ch 3, *sh in next dc**, dc in next dc; rep from * around, ending last rep at **, join with sl st in top of beg ch-3—6 shs.

RND 3: Beg sh in first st, *sh in next ch-2 sp**, sh in next dc; rep from * around, ending last rep at **, join with sl st in top of beg puff st—12 shs.

RND 4: Sl st in next ch-2 sp, beg inc sh in first ch-2 sp, *sh in next ch-2 sp**, inc sh in next ch-2 sp; rep from * around, ending last rep at **, join with sl st in top of beg puff st—6 shs; 6 inc shs.

RND 5: Sl st in next ch-2 sp, beg sh in first ch-2 sp, *sh in next ch-2 sp, inc sh in next ch-2 sp**, sh in next ch-2 sp; rep from * around, ending last rep at **, join with sl st in top of beg puff st—12 shs; 6 inc shs.

RND 6: Sl st in next ch-2 sp, beg inc sh in first ch-2 sp, *sh in each of next 3 next ch-2 sps**, inc sh in next ch-2 sp; rep from * around, ending last rep at **, join with sl st in top of beg puff st—18 shs; 6 inc shs.

RNDS 7–9: Sl st in next ch-2 sp, beg sh in first ch-2 sp, sh in each ch-2 sp around, join with sl st in top of beg puff st—30 shs.

RND 10: Sl st in next ch-2 sp, beg sh in first ch-2 sp, sh in next ch-2 sp, *inc sh in next ch-2 sp**, sh in each of next 9 ch-2 sps; rep from * around, ending last rep at **, sh in each of last 7 ch-2 sps, join with sl st in top of beg puff st—27 shs; 3 inc shs.

RNDS 11–12: Sl st in next ch-2 sp, beg sh in first ch-2 sp, sh in each ch-2 sp around, sl st in top of beg puff st—33 shs.

RND 13: Sl st in next ch-2 sp, beg inc sh in first ch-2 sp, *sh in each of next 10 ch-2 sps**, inc sh in next ch-2 sp; rep from * around, ending last rep at **, join with sl st in top of beg puff st—30 shs; 3 inc shs.

RND 14: Sl st in next ch-2 sp, beg sh in first ch-2 sp, sh in each ch-2 sp around, sl st in top of beg puff st—36 shs.

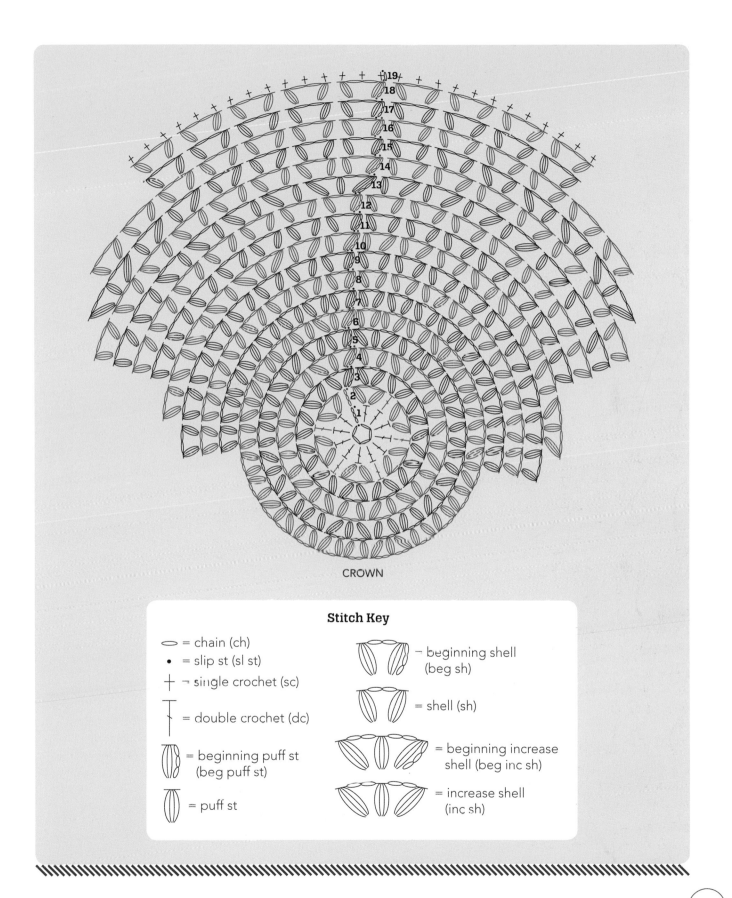

CROWN

Stitch Key

◯ = chain (ch)

• = slip st (sl st)

✝ ¬ single crochet (sc)

🇹 = double crochet (dc)

= beginning puff st (beg puff st)

= puff st

⌐ beginning shell (beg sh)

= shell (sh)

= beginning increase shell (beg inc sh)

= increase shell (inc sh)

RND 15: Sl st in next ch-2 sp, beg sh in first ch-2 sp, sh in each of next 5 ch-2 sps, *inc sh in next ch-2 sp**, sh in each of next 11 ch-2 sps; rep from * around, ending last rep at **, sh in each of next 5 ch-2 sps, join with sl st in top of beg puff st—33 shs; 3 inc shs.

RNDS 16–18: Sl st in next ch-2 sp, beg sh in first ch-2 sp, sh in each ch-2 sp around, sl st in top of beg puff st—39 shs.

RND 19: Ch 1, *sc in puff st, sc in next ch-2 sp, sc in next puff st; rep from * around, join with sl st in first sc—117 sc.

Cap Band

RNDS 20–24: Ch 1, sc in each sc around, join with sl st in first sc. Fasten off.

Visor

ROW 1: Sk first 28 sts, join yarn in next st, ch 1, sc in first 2 sts, *2 sc in next sts, [sc in each of next 3 sts] twice, 2 sc

in next st, sc in each of next 2 sts; rep from * 4 times, 2 sc in next st, sc in each of next 2 sts, turn, leaving rem sts unworked—76 sc worked over center 60 sts.

ROW 2: Ch 1, sk first st, sc in each st across to last 2 sts, sc2tog over last 2 sts, turn—74 sts.

ROWS 3–14: Rep Row 2—50 sts at end of last row.

Edging

RND 1 (RS): Ch 1, sc evenly around entire edge of cap, join with sl st in first sc. Fasten off.

Finishing

Weave in ends. Block Visor.

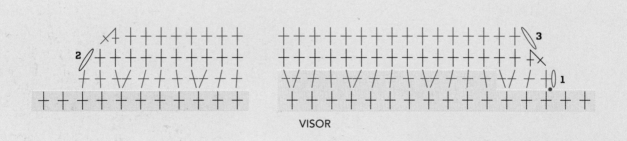

VISOR

Stitch Key

⌾ = chain (ch)

• = slip st (sl st)

+ = single crochet (sc)

⋏ = single crochet 2 together (sc2tog)

Note: The shaded area represents the last round of the Hat Band.

CHAPTER 3

A *Brave New* BOHO

Bohemian style is all about how you feel while wearing clothes rather than the clothes themselves. These playful pieces are for free spirits who love natural fibers. Textures give visual interest, and colors are earthy—just the things to keep a lyrical soul from getting weighed down.

Finished Size

21" (53.5 cm) in circumference at ribbing, stretches to fit most.

Yarn

Sportweight (#2 Fine).

Shown here: Mirasol Yarns Nuna (40% merino wool, 40% silk, 20% bamboo; 191 yd [175 m]/1¾ oz [50 g]): #15 flax (MC), 2 skeins; #25 aquamarine (CC), 1 skein. Yarn distributed by Knitting Fever.

Hook

Size G/6 (4 mm). *Adjust hook size if necessary to obtain correct gauge.*

Notions

68 beads (the sample shown uses a combination of 6 mm beads and size 6 seed beads) with holes large enough to be threaded on yarn; beading needle with eye large enough to accommodate yarn; yarn needle.

Gauge

22 sts and 16 rows = 4" (10 cm) in main pattern stitch (Rows 2–5 of Crown).

Note

To incorporate beads in your hdc, start with WS facing and all the beads you'll need threaded onto the yarn. Slide first bead down to touch work, yo, and work hdc as usual. This will secure the bead onto the right side of the work.

Gypsy SLOUCH

This slouchy cap is the perfect accessory to any bohemian ensemble. Its lacy texture and subtle beading lend a feeling of luxury. The contrasting stripe looks almost like a beaded headband and is an easy introduction to adding beads to your crochet. Worked in a lightweight wool, silk, and bamboo yarn, this hat has beautiful drape.

DESIGNED BY *Beth Nielsen*

Stitch Guide

Puff St: (Yo, insert hook in next st or sp, yo, draw yarn through and up to level of work) 4 times in same st or sp, yo, draw yarn through 9 loops on hook.

Main Stitch Pattern (patt)

RND 1: Ch 2 (counts as hdc), hdc in each st or sp across, join with sl st in top of beginning ch-2.

RND 2: Ch 3 (counts as hdc, ch 1), skip next st, *hdc in hdc, ch 1, sk next st; rep from * around, join with a sl st in 2nd ch of beg ch-3.

RND 3: Ch 2 (does not count as a st), (puff st, ch 1) in each ch-1 sp around, join with a sl st in first puff st.

RND 4: Sl st in next ch-1 sp, ch 3 (counts as hdc, ch 1), [hdc, ch 1] in each ch-1 sp around, join with a sl st in 2nd ch of beg ch-3.

Rep Rnds 1–4 for patt.

Slouch

Ribbing

With MC, ch 6.

ROW 1: Sc in 2nd ch from hook and in each ch across—5 sc, turn.

ROW 2: Ch 1, sc in blo of each sc across, turn.

ROWS 3–102: Rep Row 2.

Sl st Row 102 to foundation ch to form the ribbing in a band. Turn the band horizontally to work in the edges of each row of ribbing.

Crown

RND 1 (RS): Ch 1, sc in each row-end st around, join with sl st to first sc—102 sc.

RND 2 (INC RND): Ch 2 (counts as hdc), hdc in next sc, 2 hdc in next sc, *hdc in next 2 sc**, 2 hdc in next sc; rep from *

around, ending last rep at **, join with sl st in top of beginning ch-2—136 hdc.

RND 3: Ch 3 (counts as hdc, ch 1), skip next st, *hdc in next hdc, ch 1, sk next st; rep from * around, join with a sl st in 2nd ch of beg ch-3—68 ch-1 sps.

RND 4: Ch 2 (does not count as a st), (puff st, ch 1) in each ch-1 sp around, join with a sl st in first puff st—68 puff sts.

RND 5: Sl st in next ch-1 sp, ch 3 (counts as hdc, ch 1), [hdc, ch 1] in each ch-1 sp around, join with a sl st in 2nd ch of beg ch-3—34 ch-1 sps. Fasten off MC.

RND 6: With RS facing, join CC with sl st in first st, ch 1, sc in first st, sc in ch-1 sp and each hdc around, join with sl st to first sc.

RND 7: Ch 1, working from left to right, rev sc (see Glossary) in each sc around, join with sl st in first rev sc.

RND 8: Ch 2 (does not count as a st), BPhdc (see Glossary) in each rev sc around, join with sl st in first BPhdc. Fasten off CC.

Alternating large and small beads, string all 68 beads onto CC yarn with beading needle.

RND 9: With WS facing, join CC with sl st in first BPhdc, ch 2 (counts as hdc), *hdc with bead in next st (as per instructions in Note)**, hdc in next st; rep from * around, ending last rep at **, join with sl st in top of beg ch-2, turn.

RND 10 (RS): Ch 3 (counts as dc), dc in each st around, join with sl st in top of ch-3.

RND 11: Ch 1, working from left to right, rev sc in each dc around, join with sl st in first rev sc.

RND 12: Ch 1, BPsc (see Glossary) in each rev sc around, join with sl st in first BPsc. Fasten off CC.

With RS facing, join MC with sl st in first st.

RNDS 13–16: Work Rnds 1–4 of patt.

RND 17 (DEC RND): Ch 2 (counts as hdc), *hdc in next ch-1 sp, hdc2tog (see Glossary) over next hdc and next ch-1 sp**, hdc in next hdc; rep from * around, ending last rep at **, join with sl st in top of beg ch-2, turn—102 hdc.

RNDS 18–32: Starting with Rnd 2, work even in patt, ending with Rnd 4 of patt.

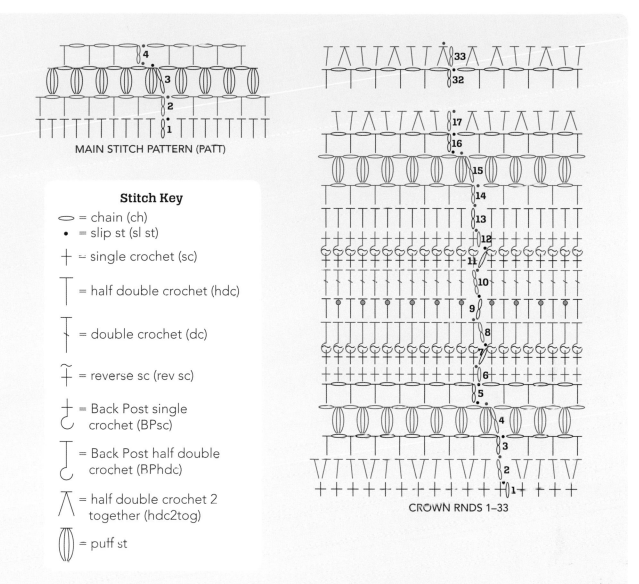

MAIN STITCH PATTERN (PATT)

Stitch Key

◯ = chain (ch)

• = slip st (sl st)

╪ = single crochet (sc)

T = half double crochet (hdc)

Ŧ = double crochet (dc)

T̃ = reverse sc (rev sc)

⊥⌒ = Back Post single crochet (BPsc)

T⌒ = Back Post half double crochet (BPhdc)

⋀ = half double crochet 2 together (hdc2tog)

⦙ = puff st

CROWN RNDS 1–33

RND 33 (DEC RND): Ch 2 (does not count as a st), hdc2tog worked in first st and next ch-1 sp, *hdc in next ch-1 sp, hdc in next hdc, hdc2tog over next hdc and next ch-1 sp; rep from * around to last 2 sts, hdc2tog over last hdc and last ch-1 sp, join with sl st in top of first hdc2tog, turn—76 hdc.

RNDS 34–37: Starting with Rnd 2, work even in patt, ending with Rnd 1 of patt. Fasten off, leaving a 15" (38 cm) tail.

Finishing

With yarn needle and 15" (38 cm) tail, weave tail through last rnd of st at top of Crown, gather tightly to close hole. Sew a few sts across the hole to secure. Fasten off. Weave in ends. Steam block lightly.

Finished Sizes

33 (36, 39)" (84 [91, 99] cm) bust circumference. Shown in size 33" (84 cm).

Yarn

Sportweight (#2 Fine).

Shown here: Louet North America Euroflax Sport (100% wet spun long linen; 650 yd [594 m]/8 oz [225 g]): #18.2464 cedarwood, 1 (1, 2) cones.

Hook

Size D/3 (3 mm). *Adjust hook size if necessary to obtain correct gauge.*

Notions

Stitch markers (m); yarn needle.

Gauge

22 sts and 8 rows = 4" (10 cm) in pattern stitch.

Note

Construction starts at the bottom, is worked in joined rounds, and then is separated for front and back starting at the armhole. Front and back shoulder will be joined with crochet on the last row.

Sienna TOP

This airy top is perfect for layering over a shirt or bikini top. The simple shaping and loose fit, bottom-up construction in one piece, and interesting pattern stitch make this a fun and easy project to crochet. Stitch up several in different colors or just add length to create a tunic or even a swingy dress.

DESIGNED BY *Mimi Alelis*

Stitch Guide

3-tr Cluster (3-tr cl): [Yo twice, insert hook in next st, yo, draw up a lp, (yo, draw yarn through 2 lps on hook) twice] 3 times, yo, draw yarn through 4 loops on hook.

4-tr Cluster (4-tr cl): [Yo twice, insert hook in next st, yo, draw up a lp, (yo, draw yarn through 2 lps on hook) twice] 4 times, yo, draw yarn through 5 loops on hook.

Stitch Pattern in Rnds (Patt in Rnds)

Ch a multiple of 4, join with sl st in the first ch.

Rnd 1 (RS): Ch 1 (does not count as a st), hdc in each ch around, join with sl st in first hdc.

Rnd 2 (RS): Ch 4, 3-tr cl over next 3 hdc, *ch 5, 4-tr cl over next 4 hdc; rep from * around, ending with ch 2, dc on top of first 3-tr cl instead of last ch-5 sp, turn—46 (50, 54) cl.

Rnd 3 (WS): Ch 1, sc in first sp, (ch 5, sc) in each ch-5 loop around, ending with ch 2, dc on top of first sc instead of last ch-5 sp, turn.

Rnd 4 (RS): Ch 4 (counts as tr here and throughout), 3 tr in top of dc of last sp, 4 dc in center ch of each ch-5 loop around, join with sl st in top of beg ch-4, turn.

Rnd 5 (RS): Ch 1, hdc in each tr around, turn.

Rep Rnds 2–5 for Patt in Rnds.

Stitch Pattern in Rows (Patt in Rows)

Ch a multiple of 4 plus 3.

Row 1 (WS): Hdc in 2nd ch from hook and on each ch across, turn.

Row 2 (RS): Ch 6 (counts as tr, ch 2 here and throughout), 4-tr cl over next 4 hdc, *ch 5, 4-tr cl over next 4 hdc; rep from * across to last st, ch 2, tr in last st, turn.

Row 3: Ch 1, sc in first tr, (ch 5, sc) in each ch-5 loop across to last ch-5 sp, ch 5, sc in 4th ch of beg ch-6, turn.

Row 4: Ch 4 (counts as tr here and throughout), 4 tr in center ch of each ch-5 loop across, tr in the last st, turn.

Row 5: Ch 1, hdc in each tr across, hdc on top of beg ch-4, turn.

Rep Rows 2–5 for Patt in Rows.

Body

Ch 184 (200, 216), join with sl st in the first ch.

RND 1 (RS): Ch 1 (does not count as a st), hdc in each ch around, join with sl st in first hdc—184 (200, 216) hdc.

Work even in Patt in Rnds for 9 (9, 13) more rnds.

RND 11 (15) (WS): Ch 1, sc in first sp, (ch 5, sc) in each ch-5 loop around, ending with ch 5, join with sl st in first sc, turn—46 (50, 54) ch-5 sps. Place marker (m) on this st to mark the middle of underarm. Place another m on the sc at the opposite side of this row to mark the middle of the other underarm.

RND 12 (16) (INC ROW): Sl st in each of next 2 ch, ch 4, 3 tr in the same st, sk next ch, 4 tr in next ch (inc made), 4 dc in center ch of each of next 21 (23, 25) ch-5 loops, [4 tr in

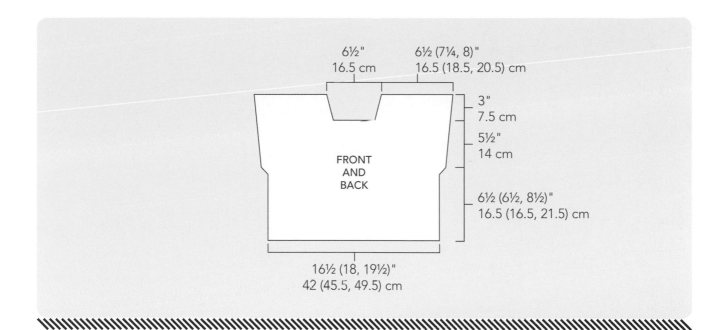

6½"
16.5 cm

6½ (7¼, 8)"
16.5 (18.5, 20.5) cm

3"
7.5 cm

5½"
14 cm

FRONT
AND
BACK

6½ (6½, 8½)"
16.5 (16.5, 21.5) cm

16½ (18, 19½)"
42 (45.5, 49.5) cm

2nd ch of next loop, sk next ch, 4 tr in next ch] twice, 4 dc in center ch of each of next 21 (23, 25) ch-5 loops, 4 tr in 2nd ch of next loop, sk next ch, 4 tr in next ch, sl st in top of beg ch-4, turn—200 (216, 232) tr.

RND 13 (17): Work Rnd 5 of Patt in Rnds. Do not fasten off.

Note: Work will now be separated for Front and Back and will be worked in rows.

Front

ROW 1: Ch 6 (counts as tr, ch 2), starting in same hdc, 4-tr cl over first 4 hdc, *ch 5, 4-tr cl over next 4 hdc; rep from * 23 (25, 27) times, ch 2, tr in same hdc as last tr of cl, turn—25 (27, 29) cl.

ROW 2: Ch 1, sc in first tr, (ch 5, sc) in each ch-5 loop across to last ch-5 sp, ch 5, sc in 4th ch of beg ch-6, turn—25 (27, 29) ch-5 sps.

ROW 3: Ch 4, 3 tr in first sc (inc made), 4 tr in center ch of each ch-5 loop across, 4 tr in the last st, turn—108 (116, 124) tr.

ROW 4: Ch 1, hdc in each tr across, hdc on top of beg ch-4, turn—108 (116, 124) hdc.

Starting with Row 2, work even in Patt in Rows for 6 rows, ending with Row 3 of patt.

Shape Front Neck

ROW 11: Ch 4, 4 tr in center ch of each of next 10 (11, 12) ch-5 sps, ch 4, 4 hdc in each of next 7 ch-5 sps, ch 4, 4 tr in center ch of each of next 10 (11, 12) ch-5 sps, tr in the last sc, turn.

Note: Work will now be separate for Right Front And Left Front up to shoulder.

Right Front

ROW 1 (WS): Ch 1 (does not count as a st), hdc in each of first 41 (45, 49) tr, turn, leaving rem sts unworked.

ROW 2: Ch 4, 3-tr cl over next 3 hdc, *ch 5, 4-tr cl over next 4 hdc; rep from * across, ch 2, tr in the last st, turn—10 (11, 12) cl.

ROW 3: Ch 1, sc in the same st, (ch 5, sc) in each of next 9 (10, 11) ch-5 sps, turn—9 (10, 11) ch-5 sps.

ROW 4: Ch 4 (does not count as a st), 4 tr in the center ch of each ch-5 loop across, tr in the last sc, turn—37 (41, 45) tr.

ROW 5: Ch 1, hdc in each tr across, do not work in tch, turn—37 (41, 45) hdc.

ROW 6: Ch 4, 3-tr cl over next 3 hdc, *ch 5, 4-tr cl over next 4 hdc; rep from * across, ch 2, tr in the last st—9 (10, 11) cl. Fasten off.

Left Front

ROW 1: With WS facing, sk center 28 hdc at neck, join yarn in first tr on Left Front, ch 1, hdc in same st, hdc in each st across, turn—41 (45, 49) hdc.

ROW 2: Ch 6 (counts as tr, ch 2), 4-tr cl over next 4 hdc, *ch 5, 4-tr cl over next 4 hdc; rep from * across, turn—10 (11, 12) cl.

ROW 3: Sl st in next 2 ch, ch 1, sc in next ch, (ch 5, sc) in each ch-5 sp across, ending with ch 5, sc on top of beg ch-4, turn—9 (10, 11) ch-5 sps.

ROW 4: Ch 4 (does not count as a st), 4 tr in center ch of each ch-5 sp across, tr in the last sc, turn—37 (41, 45) tr.

ROW 5: Ch 1, hdc in same st, hdc in each tr across, turn—37 (41, 45) hdc.

ROW 6: Ch 6, 4-tr cl over next 4 hdc, *ch 5, 4-tr cl over next 4 hdc; rep from * across—9 (10, 11) cl. Fasten off.

Back
Shape Back Neck

ROW 11: With RS facing, join yarn in marked st at right underarm, ch 4, 4 tr in center ch of each of next 10 (11, 12) ch-5 sps, ch 4, 4 hdc in each of next 7 ch-5 sps, ch 4, 4 tr in center ch of each of next 10 (11, 12) ch-5 sps, tr in the last sc, turn.

Note: Work will now be separate for Left Back and Right Back up to shoulder.

Left Back

Work same as Right Front through Row 5.

ROW 6: Ch 6, 4-tr cl over next 4 hdc, *ch 2, sc in corresponding ch-5 sp on Right Front shoulder, 4-tr cl over next 4 hdc; rep from * across—9 (10, 11) cl. Fasten off.

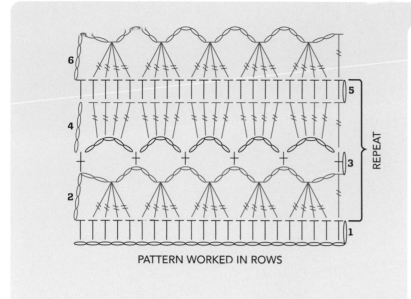

PATTERN WORKED IN ROWS

Stitch Key

$\bigcirc$ = chain (ch)

$\bullet$ = slip st (sl st)

$+$ = single crochet (sc)

$\top$ = half double crochet (hdc)

$\dagger$ = double crochet (dc)

$\ddagger$ = treble crochet (tr)

= 3-tr cluster (3-tr cl)

= 4-tr cluster (4-tr cl)

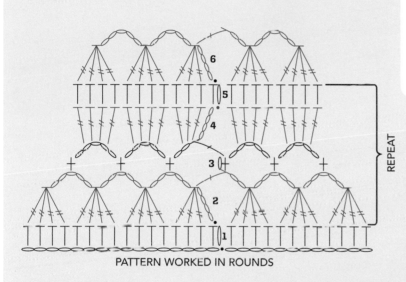

PATTERN WORKED IN ROUNDS

Right Back

Work same as Left Front through Row 5.

ROW 6: Ch 6, 4-tr cl over next 4 hdc, *ch 2, sc in corresponding ch-5 sp on Left Front shoulder, 4-tr cl over next 4 hdc; rep from * across—9 (10, 11) cl. Fasten off.

Finishing

Weave in ends. Block.

Finished Size

Tote measures 12½" wide × 14" tall (31.5 × 35.5 cm). Strap measures 2¼" wide × 40" long (5.5 × 101.5 cm).

Yarn

Fingering weight (#1 Super Fine).

Shown here: Brown Sheep Cotton Fine (80% cotton, 20% wool (222 yd [203 m]/1¾ oz [50 g]): CW100, cotton ball (A), CW460 jungle green (B), CW345 gold dust (C), one skein each.

Hook

Size D/3 (3.25 mm). *Adjust hook size if necessary to obtain correct gauge.*

Gauge

20 sts and 14 rows in pattern = 4" (10 cm).

Greenwich Village
TOTE

This hard-working tote could go just about anywhere. It's durable enough to be a book bag, fashionable enough to carry around as a project bag, and just the right size for taking to the farmer's market on Saturday morning.

DESIGNED BY *Yoko Hatta*

Tote

With A, ch 65.

RND 1 (RS): Sc in 2nd ch from hook, sc in each of next 3 ch, *dc in each of next 8 ch, sc in each of next 8 ch*; rep from * to * 6 times, sc in each of next 3 ch, 2 sc in last ch, working across opposite side of foundation ch, sc in each of next 3 ch; rep from * to * 6 times, sc in each of next 4 ch, join with sl st in first sc, turn.

RND 2 (WS): Ch 3 (counts as dc here and throughout), dc in each of next 4 sc, *sc in each of next 8 dc, dc in each of next 8 sc*; rep from * around, ending with dc in each of last 3 sc, join with sl st in top of beg ch-3, turn.

RND 3: Ch 1, sc in each of first 4 dc, *dc in each of next 8 sc, sc in each of next 8 dc; rep from * around, ending with sc in each of next 4 ch, join with sl st in first sc, turn.

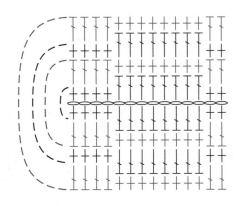

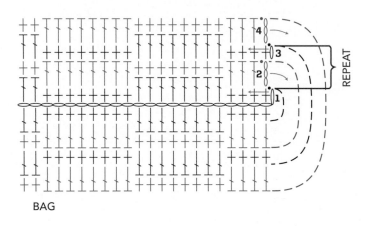

BAG

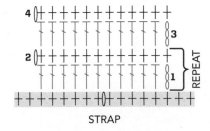

STRAP

Note: The shaded area represents the last round of the Tote.

Stitch Key

⌒ = chain (ch)

• = slip st (sl st)

+ = single crochet (sc)

T = double crochet (dc)

RNDS 4–48: Rep Rnds 2–3 for pattern, working in the following color sequence: 2 more rnds A, *1 rnd each of B, C, and A; rep from * 12 times, 4 rnds A.

RND 49 (RS): Ch 1, sc in each st around, join with sl st in first sc, turn.

RND 50 (WS): Rep Rnd 49. Fasten off.

Strap

ROW 1: With RS facing, join A in 6th st to the left of join in last Rnd of Tote, ch 3, dc in each of next 11 sc, turn—12 dc.

ROW 2: Ch 1, sc in each dc across, turn.

ROW 3: Ch 3, dc in each sc across, turn.

ROWS 4–114: Rep Rows 2–3 (55 times), rep Row 2 once. Fasten off A, join C in first st.

ROW 115: With C, rep Row 3.

ROWS 116–124: Rep Rows 2–3, working 3 more rows C, 4 rows B, 2 rows A. Fasten off, leaving a sewing length.

Finishing

Without twisting Strap, sew last row of Strap to corresponding 12 sts on opposite side of Tote. Weave in ends.

Finished Size

7½" (19 cm) in circumference around palm; 8½" (21.5 cm) long.

Yarn

Sportweight (#2 Fine).

Shown here: Valley Yarns Northampton Sport (100% wool; 164 yd [150 m]/1¾ oz [50 g]: burgundy, 2 hanks. Yarn distributed by WEBS.

Hook

Size D/3 (3.25 mm). *Adjust hook size if necessary to obtain correct gauge.*

Notions

Yarn needle.

Gauge

20 sts and 10 rows dc = 4" (10 cm).

Note

Mittens are worked in joined rnds, turning at the end of each rnd. Thumbs are worked later into thumb openings.

Montmartre MITTENS

The cables and bobbles in these mittens add just the right amount of bulk and warmth to withstand the coldest days of winter. The superwash wool keeps them practical, but they're charming enough to wear on a stroll around a Parisian *arrondissement*.

DESIGNED BY *Yoko Hatta*

Stitch Guide

Double Crochet 2 Together (dc2tog): *Yo, insert hook in next st, pull up lp, yo, draw through 2 lps; rep from * once in designated st, yo, draw through 3 lps.

BPdc/dctog: Yo, insert hook from back to front to back around the post of next st, pull up lp, yo, draw through 2 lps, yo, insert hook in top of next st, yo, pull up lp, yo, draw through 2 lps, yo, draw through 3 lps.

dc/BPdctog: Yo, insert hook in top of next st, yo, pull up lp, yo, draw through 2 lps, yo, insert hook from back to front to back around the post of next st, pull up lp, yo, draw through 2 lps, yo, draw through 3 lps.

FPdc2tog: *Yo, insert hook from front to back to front around the post of next st, pull up lp, yo, draw through 2 lps; rep from * once, yo, draw through 3 lps.

3-dc Cluster (3-dc cl): [Yo, insert hook in indicated st, yo and pull up lp, yo, draw through 2 lps] 3 times in same sp, yo, draw through 4 on hook.

Left Mitten

Ch 38, without twisting ch, join with sl st in first ch.

RND 1 (RS): Ch 3 (counts as dc, here and throughout, unless otherwise noted), sk first ch, dc in each ch around, join with sl st in top of beg ch-3, turn—38 dc.

RND 2 (WS): Ch 3, dc in each of next 21 dc, BPdc (see Glossary) in each of next 2 sts, dc in each of next 3 sts, sk next st, BPdc in each of next 2 sts, working in front of last 2 post sts, dc in last skipped st, sk next 2 sts, dc in next st, working behind last dc made, BPdc in each of last 2 skipped sts, dc in each of next 3 sts, BPdc in each of next 2 sts, join with sl st in top of beg ch-3, turn—38 sts.

RND 3: Ch 3, FPdc (see Glossary) in each of next 2 sts, dc in each of next 2 sts, sk next st, FPdc in each of next 2 sts, working behind last 2 post sts, dc in last skipped st, dc in each of next 2 sts, sk next 2 sts, dc in next st; working in front of last dc, FPdc in each of last 2 skipped sts, dc in each of next 2 sts, FPdc in each of next 2 sts, dc in each of next 21 sts, join with sl st in top of beg ch-3, turn.

RND 4: Ch 3, dc in each of next 21 dc, BPdc in each of next 2 sts, dc in next st, sk next st, BPdc in each of next 2 sts, working in front of last 2 post sts, dc in last skipped st, dc in each of next 4 sts, sk next 2 sts, dc in next st, working behind last dc made, BPdc in each of last 2 skipped sts, dc in next st, BPdc in each of next 2 sts, join with sl st in top of beg ch-3, turn.

RND 5: Ch 3, FPdc in each of next 2 sts, dc in next st, sk next 2 sts, dc in next st, working in front of last dc, FPdc in each of last 2 skipped sts, dc in each of next 2 sts, 3-dc cl in sp before next dc, dc in each of next 2 dc, sk next st, FPdc in each of next sts, working in back of last 2 post sts, dc in last skipped st, dc in next st, FPdc in each of next 2 sts, dc in each of next 21 sts, join with sl st in top of beg ch-3, turn—39 sts.

RND 6: Ch 3, dc in each of next 21 dc, BPdc in each of next 2 sts, dc in each of next 2 sts, sk next 2 sts, dc in

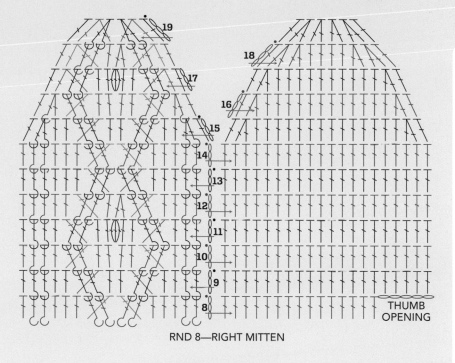

RND 8—RIGHT MITTEN

THUMB OPENING

RND 8—LEFT MITTEN

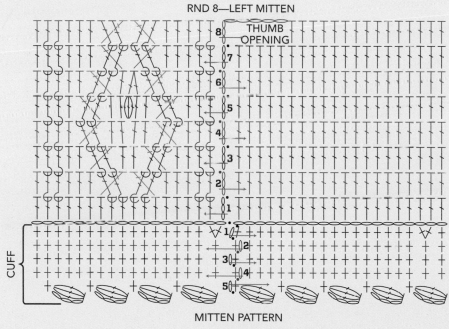

THUMB OPENING

CUFF

MITTEN PATTERN

next st, working behind last dc made, BPdc in each of last 2 skipped sts, dc in next st, dc2tog over next 2 sts, sk next st, BPdc in each of next 2 sts, working in front of last 2 post sts, dc in last skipped st, dc in next 2 sts, BPdc in each of next 2 sts, join with sl st in top of beg ch-3, turn—38 sts.

RND 7: Ch 3, FPdc in each of next 2 sts, dc in each of next 3 sts, sk next 2 sts, dc in next st, working in front of last dc, FPdc in each of last 2 skipped sts, sk next st, FPdc in each of next sts, working in back of last 2 post sts, dc in last skipped st, dc in each of next 3 sts, FPdc in each of next 2 sts, dc in each of next 21 sts, join with sl st in top of beg ch-3, turn.

RND 8 (THUMBHOLE RND): Ch 8 (counts as dc, ch 5), sk next 5 sts, (thumbhole made), dc in each of next 16 sts, BPdc in each of next 2 sts, dc in each of next 3 sts, sk next st, BPdc in each of next 2 sts, working in front of last 2 post sts, dc in last skipped st, sk next 2 sts, dc in next st, working behind last dc, BPdc in each of last 2 skipped sts, BPdc in each of next 2 sts, join with sl st in top of beg ch-3, turn.

RNDS 9–13: Rep Rnds 3–7.

RND 14: Rep Rnd 2.

RND 15: Ch 3 (does not count as a st for remainder of Mitten), dc in first st, FPdc2tog over next 2 sts, dc in each of next 2 sts, sk next st, FPdc in each of next 2 sts, working behind post st, dc in last skipped st, dc in each of next 2 sts, skip next 2 sts, dc in next st, working in front of last dc, FPdc in each of last 2 skipped sts, dc in each of next 2 sts, FPdc2tog over next 2 sts, dc in each of next 2 sts, dc2tog over next 2 sts, dc in each of next 14 st, dc2tog over next 2 sts, dc in last st, join with sl st in top of beg ch-3, turn—34 sts.

RND 16: Ch 3, dc in next st, dc2tog over next 2 sts, dc in each of next 12 sts, dc2tog over next 2 sts, dc in each of next 2 sts, BPdc/dctog over next 2 sts, sk next st, BPdc in each of next 2 sts, working in front of last 2 post sts, dc in last skipped st, dc in each of next 4 sts, sk next 2 sts, dc in next st, working behind last dc, BPdc in each of last 2 skipped sts, dc/BPdctog over next 2 sts, dc in last st, join with sl st in top of beg ch-3, turn—30 sts.

RND 17: Ch 3, dc in next st, dc2tog, working first leg in next st, sk next 2 sts, work 2nd leg in next st, complete

dc2tog, working in front of last leg of dc2tog, FPdc in each of last 2 skipped sts, dc in each of next 2 sts, 3-dc cl in sp before next dc, dc in each of next 2 dc, sk next st, FPdc in each of next 2 sts, working behind last 2 post sts, work dc2tog, working first leg of dc2tog in last skipped st, work 2nd dc in next st after 2 post sts, complete dc2tog, dc in each of next 2 sts, dc2tog over next 2 sts, dc in each of next 10 sts, dc2tog over next 2 sts, dc in last st, join with sl st in top of beg ch-3, turn—27 sts.

RND 18: Ch 3, dc in next st, [dc2tog over next 2 sts] twice, dc in each of next 4 sts, [dc2tog over next 2 sts] twice, dc in each of next 3 sts, dc2tog, working first leg in next st, sk next 2 sts, work 2nd leg in next st, complete dc2tog, BPdc in each of last 2 skipped sts, dc in next st, dc2tog over next 2 sts, sk next st, BPdc in each of next 2 sts, working behind last 2 post sts, work dc2tog, working first leg of dc2tog in last skipped st, work 2nd dc in next st after 2 post sts, complete dc2tog, dc in last st, join with sl st in top of beg ch-3, turn—20 sts.

RND 19: Ch 3, dc in next st, dc2tog, working first leg in next st, sk next 2 sts, work 2nd leg in next st, complete dc2tog, working in front of last leg of dc2tog, FPdc2tog in next 2 sts, sk next st, FPdc2tog in next 2 sts, working behind last FPdc2tog, dc2tog, working first leg of dc2tog in last skipped st, work 2nd dc in next st after FPdc2tog, complete dc2tog, dc in each of next 2 sts, [dc2tog over next 2 sts] 4 times, dc in last st, join with sl st in top of beg ch-3, turn—27 sts. Fasten off, leaving a sewing length. With yarn needle, weave sewing length through sts of last rnd, gather and secure.

Cuff

RND 1: With RS facing, working across opposite side of foundation ch, join yarn in any ch, ch 1, starting in same ch, sc in first 17 sts, sc2tog over next 2 ch, sc in each of next 17 ch, sc2tog over next 2 ch, join with sl st in first sc, turn—36 sts.

RNDS 2–4: Ch 1, sc in each st around, join with sl st in first sc, turn.

RND 5 (RS): Ch 1, sc in first st, ch 3, 3-dc cl working in side of last sc made, sk next 3 sts, *sc in next st, ch 3, 3-dc cl working in side of last sc made; rep from * around, join with sl st in first sc, turn—9 clusters.

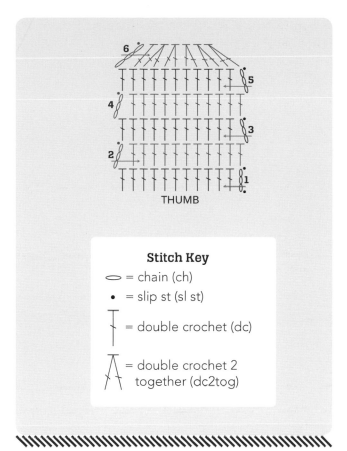

THUMB

Stitch Key

⬭ = chain (ch)

• = slip st (sl st)

⊤ = double crochet (dc)

⋀ = double crochet 2
together (dc2tog)

Thumb

RND 1: With RS of 1 Mitten facing, join yarn in top of first skipped st in Row 7 for thumbhole, ch 3 (counts as dc here and throughout), dc in each of next 4 dc, dc in next row-end st in Rnd 8, working across opposite side of ch-5 sp, dc in each of next 5 ch, dc in next row-end st in Rnd 8, join with sl st in top of beg ch-3, turn—12 dc.

RNDS 2–5: Ch 3, dc in each dc around, join with sl st in top of beg ch-3, turn.

Note: *For longer thumb, work 1 more rnd of dc.*

RND 6: Ch 3, dc in next dc, [dc2tog over next 2 sts] 5 times, join with sl st in top of beg ch-3—7 sts. Fasten off, leaving a sewing length. With yarn needle, weave sewing length through sts of last rnd, gather and secure.

Right Mitten

Work same as Left Mitten through Rnd 7.

RND 8 (THUMBHOLE RND): Ch 3, dc in each of next 15 sts, ch 5, sk next 5 sts, (thumbhole made), dc in next st, BPdc in each of next 2 sts, dc in each of next 3 sts, sk next st, BPdc in each of next 2 sts, working in front of last 2 post sts, dc in last skipped st, sk next 2 sts, dc in next st, working behind last dc, BPdc in each of last 2 skipped sts, BPdc in each of next 2 sts, join with sl st in top of beg ch-3, turn.

Complete same as Left Mitten.

Finished Size

Directions are given for size Small (S). Changes for Medium (M) and Large (L) are in parentheses. Length of stockings can easily be changed and is noted in pattern. Stockings measure 9½ (10¼, 11)" (24 [26, 28] cm) around calf; 6¾ (7½, 8¼)" (17 [19, 21] cm) around narrowest part of ankle; 6¼ (7, 7¾)" (16 [18, 19.5] cm) around foot. Stockings are stretchy and are designed to be worn with 3½–5" (9–12.5 cm) of negative ease at calf. Stockings measure 9" (23 cm) from corner of heel to tip of toe; 15" (38 cm) from corner of heel to top edge of stocking. Stockings fit US Women's shoe sizes 8–11. Notes for shortening or lengthening (the foot and/or calf length) are written in pattern. Sample shown is size M.

Yarn

Fingering weight (#1 Super Fine).

Shown here: Misti Alpaca Tonos Carnival (50% alpaca, 30% merino wool, 10% silk, 10% nylon; 436 yd [400 m]/3½ oz [100 g]): #TF04 chestnut, 2 skeins.

Hooks

Sizes C/2 (2.75 mm) and B/1 (2.25 mm). *Adjust hook sizes if necessary to obtain correct gauge.*

Notions

Stitch markers (m); yarn needle.

Gauge

30 sts and 56 rows = 4" (10 cm) in sl st in blo with smaller hook. 30 sts and 36 rows = 4" (10 cm) in main st patt with smaller hook (see Stitch Guide). Rows 1–10 of pineapple motif pattern (worked with larger hook) measures about 4½" (11.5 cm) long. Finished pineapple motif measures about 12" (30.5 cm) long × 4" (10 cm) wide (at widest point).

Bon Vivant
STOCKINGS

The pineapple motif ingeniously decorates the back of these lacy stockings to create the shaping needed for the calf. Rows of slip stitch worked through the back loops alternate with rows of double crochet to allow for an elastic, comfortable fit. The heel and toe are worked last, making it easy to replace these areas after they wear out.

DESIGNED BY *Brenda K. B. Anderson*

Notes

A series of short rows shape the heel gusset. You do not need to know how to work short rows—this will be explained in the pattern. Each stocking requires one sl st seam (see Glossary) along the side of stocking and a short seam to close the toe and heel.

These stockings are constructed in this order: First the sl st sole is made, and then the pineapple lace motif is created. Vertical rows are worked from the center back motif outward to the left and right sides of the motif, joining the sl st sole as you work. The heel and toe are worked in joined rnds.

Working in the sl st pattern is much easier if you intentionally make sts a little bit loose. Otherwise, you will find it difficult to get your hook in each st. Pull up on each st just a little more than you normally would to keep them from getting too tight. When counting rows worked in sl st in blo pattern, it can be difficult to count rows. If you stretch the fabric slightly, you will see a series of ridges. Each ridge is made of 2 rows. For example, if you see 3 ridges, you have worked 6 rows.

Dc sts and Ldc are only worked on RS rows. (This will help count sl st rows.)

If you are trying to decide whether to shorten the foot, it's better to make it too short than too long. You can always add length to the foot later when working the toe section.

Stitch Guide

Beginning Shell (beg sh): Ch 3, (2 dc, ch 2, 3 dc) in same sp.

Shell (sh): (3 dc, ch 2, 3 dc) in same sp.

Linked Double Crochet (Ldc): To make a Ldc when previous st is a turning ch: Insert hook from right to left in flo of 2nd ch from hook, yo, draw through lp (2 lps on hook), insert hook in blo of same st as join, yo, draw yarn through st (3 lps on hook), [yo and draw through 2 lps] twice—1 Ldc made. To make a Ldc when previous st is a Ldc or dc: Insert hook from top to bottom through the horizontal bar of the previous st, yo, draw yarn through lp (2 lps on hook), insert hook in blo of next st, yo, draw yarn through st (3 lps on hook), [yo and draw through 2 lps on hook] twice—Ldc made.

Puff Stitch (puff st): [Yo, insert hook in next ch-2 sp, yo, draw up lp to level of work] 3 times in same sp, yo, draw through all 7 lps on hook.

Main Stitch Pattern

To make gauge swatch: Ch 32, turn.

ROW 1 (WS): Working in the bottom ridges of ch sts, sl st in 2nd ch from hook and in each ch across, turn—31 sl sts.

ROWS 2–5: Ch 1 (does not count as a st), sl st in blo of each st across, turn—31 sts.

ROW 6: Ch 3 (does not count as a st), dc in first st, *ch 1, sk next st, dc in next st; rep from * across, turn.

Rep Rows 2–6 for patt.

Stocking (make 2)

Sole

With smaller hook, ch 45. (To adjust sole length, add or subtract about 4 sts for every ½" [1.3 cm] of length.)

Work short-row series: Working in bottom ridges of ch sts, sl st in 2nd ch from hook and in each of next 15 ch, ch 1, turn, leaving rem sts unworked, sl st in blo of each of next 16 sts, turn, [ch 1, sl st in blo of each of next 12 sts, turn] twice, [ch 1, sl st in blo of each of next 8 sts, turn] twice, [ch 1, sl st in blo of each of next 4 sts, turn] twice.

ROW 1: Ch 1, sl st in blo of each of first 4 sts, [sl st in blo of next 4 sts 2 rows below] 3 times, sl st in blo of each rem st across, turn—44 sts.

ROWS 2–52: Ch 1, sl st in blo of each st across, turn—44 sts. You will end at the short-row (heel) edge after working Row 52.

WORK SHORT-ROW SERIES: [Ch 1, sl st in blo of each of next 4 sts, turn] twice, [ch 1, sl st in blo of each of next 8 sts, turn] twice, [ch 1, sl st in blo of each of next 12 sts, turn] twice, [ch 1, sl st in blo of each of next 16 sts, turn] twice.

ROWS 53–54: Ch 1, sl st in blo of each st across, turn—44 sts. Fasten off. Place marker (pm) in last st made. Pm on side facing when working Row 53 to mark RS.

Pineapple Motif

ROW 1 (RS): With larger hook, ch 4 (first 3 ch count as dc), (2 dc, ch 3, 3 dc) in 4th ch from hook, turn—one large sh.

ROWS 2–12: Sl st in first 3 dc, sl st in next ch-3 sp, ch 3, (2 dc, ch 3, 3 dc) in same sp—one large sh made, turn. *Note: To lengthen or shorten the length of the calf by 1" (2.5 cm), add or subtract 2 rows. For every 2 rows added or subtracted to Pineapple Motif, patt on sides will be adjusted by 7 sts.*

ROW 13 (RS): Sl st in first 3 dc, sl st in next ch-3 sp, ch 3, (2 dc, ch 2, 3 dc, ch 2, 3 dc) in same ch-3 sp, turn—9 dc, 2 ch-2 sps.

ROW 14: Sl st in first 3 dc, sl st in next ch-2 sp, beg sh in same ch-2 sp, sh in next ch-2 sp, turn—2 shs.

ROW 15: Sl st in first 3 dc, sl st in next ch-2 sp, beg sh in same ch-2 sp, dc in sp between shells of previous row, sh in next ch-2 sp, turn—2 shs; 1 dc.

ROW 16: Sl st in first 3 dc, sl st in next ch-2 sp, beg sh in same ch-2 sp, sk next 3 dc, dc in next dc, sh in next ch-2 sp, turn—2 shs; 1 dc.

ROW 17: Sl st in first 3 dc, sl st in next ch-2 sp, beg sh in same ch-2 sp, sk next 3 dc, (dc, ch 1, dc) in next dc, sh in next ch-2 sp, turn—2 shs; (dc, ch 1, dc).

ROW 18: Sl st in first 3 dc, sl st in next ch-2 sp, beg sh in same ch-2 sp, (dc, ch 3, dc) in next ch-1 sp, sh in next ch-2 sp, turn—2 shs; (dc, ch 3, dc).

ROW 19: Sl st in first 3 dc, sl st in next ch-2 sp, beg sh in same ch-2 sp, 7 dc in next ch-3 sp, sh in next ch-2 sp, turn—2 shs; 7 dc.

ROW 20: Sl st in first 3 dc, sl st in next ch-2 sp, beg sh in same ch-2 sp, sk next 3 dc, 2 dc in next dc, dc in each of next 5 dc, 2 dc in next dc, sh in next ch-2 sp, turn—2 shs; 9 dc.

ROW 21: Sl st in first 3 dc, sl st in next ch-2 sp, beg sh in same ch-2 sp, ch 1, (dc, ch 1) in each next 9 dc, sh in next ch-2 sp, turn—2 shs; 9 dc; 8 ch-1 sps.

ROW 22: Sl st in first 3 dc, sl st in next ch-2 sp, beg sh in same ch-2 sp, ch 2, sk next ch-1 sp, (puff st, ch 1) in each of next 8 ch-1 sps, ch 1 more, sh in next ch-2 sp, turn—2 shs; 8 puff sts; 7 ch-1 sps; 2 ch-2 sps.

ROW 23: Sl st in first 3 dc, sl st in next ch-2 sp, beg sh in same ch-2 sp, ch 2, sk next ch-2 sp, (puff st, ch 1) in each of next 7 ch-1 sps, ch 1 more, sk next ch-2 sp, sh in next ch-2 sp, turn—2 shs; 7 puff sts; 6 ch-1 sps; 2 ch-2 sps.

ROW 24: Sl st in first 3 dc, sl st in next ch-2 sp, beg sh in same ch-2 sp, ch 2, sk next ch-2 sp, (puff st, ch 1) in each of next 6 ch-1 sps, ch 1 more, sk next ch-2 sp, sh in next ch-2 sp, turn—2 shs; 6 puff sts; 5 ch-1 sps; 2 ch-2 sps.

ROW 25: Sl st in first 3 dc, sl st in next ch-2 sp, beg sh in same ch-2 sp, ch 2, sk next ch-2 sp, (puff st, ch 1) in each of next 5 ch-1 sps, ch 1 more, sk next ch-2 sp, sh in next ch-2 sp, turn—2 shs; 5 puff sts; 4 ch-1 sps; 2 ch-2 sps.

ROW 26: Sl st in first 3 dc, sl st in next ch-2 sp, beg sh in same ch-2 sp, ch 2, sk next ch-2 sp, (puff st, ch 1) in each of next 4 ch-1 sps, ch 1 more, sk next ch-2 sp, sh in next ch-2 sp, turn—2 shs; 4 puff sts; 3 ch-1 sps; 2 ch-2 sps.

ROW 27: Sl st in first 3 dc, sl st in next ch-2 sp, beg sh in same ch-2 sp, ch 2, sk next ch-2 sp, (puff st, ch 1) in each of next 3 ch-1 sps, ch 1 more, sk next ch-2 sp, sh in next ch-2 sp, turn—2 shs; 3 puff sts; 2 ch-1 sps; 2 ch-2 sps.

ROW 28: Sl st in first 3 dc, sl st in next ch-2 sp, beg sh in same ch-2 sp, ch 2, sk next ch-2 sp, (puff st, ch 1) in each of next 2 ch-1 sps, ch 1 more, sk next ch-2 sp, sh in next ch-2 sp, turn—2 shs; 2 puff sts; 1 ch-1 sps; 2 ch-2 sps.

ROW 29: Sl st in first 3 dc, sl st in next ch-2 sp, beg sh in same ch-2 sp, ch 2, sk next ch-2 sp, puff st in next ch-1 sp, ch 2, sk next ch-2 sp, sh in next ch-2 sp—2 shs; 1 puff st; 2 ch-2 sps. Pm to denote RS of motif.

Do not fasten off.

Begin Left Side

Place working lp on smaller hook. Ch 9.

SET-UP ROW: With RS of Pineapple Motif facing and working in bottom ridge lp of ch sts, insert hook in 2nd ch from hook, yo and pull up lp, sk next ch, insert hook in following ch, yo and pull up lp, [yo and draw through 2 lps] twice (first Ldc made), Ldc in each of next 5 ch, pm in ch at bottom of first Ldc of row (this is where you will join to beg Back Knee Ribbing later), ch 2, sk first row-end st, working in top of each row-end st on side edge, dc in next row-end st, *ch 3, dc in next row-end st, ch 2, dc in next row-end st; rep from * across to last row, ch 3, dc in last row-end st—28 ch-sps with a total of 104 sts. If you lengthened or shortened the Pineapple Motif, you will have more or fewer sts (in multiples of 7) now and throughout.

Pm in live lp to keep it from unraveling while you work the Back Knee Ribbing and Right Side of motif.

Back Knee Ribbing

Using smaller hook with WS facing, join yarn with sl st in marked ch of ribbing, and working across opposite side of foundation ch of Ribbing, ch 1, starting in first ch, *[sl st in blo of next 6 ch, sl st in next dc of sh at top of Motif, turn, sl st in blo of next 6 sts, turn, ch 1] 3 times*, [sl st in blo of next 6 sts, sl st in next ch-2 sp in sh, turn, sl st in next 6 sts, turn, ch 1] twice in same ch-2 sp, [sl st in blo of next 6 sts, ch 1, turn] 3 times, [sl st in blo of next 6 sts, sl st in ch-2 sp of next sh on opposite side of Motif, turn, sl st in next 6 sts, turn, ch 1] twice in same ch-2 sp; rep from * to * once. Fasten off, omitting last ch-1 of last rep. *Note: The last row worked was a RS row.*

Right Side

SET-UP ROW: With RS facing and smaller hook, join with sl st in top of first dc of Row 1 of Pineapple Motif, ch 3 (does not count as a st), insert hook in 2nd ch from hook, yo, draw up a lp, insert hook in same corner dc of Row 1, yo, draw up a lp, [yo, draw yarn through 2 lps on hook] twice (first Ldc made), working in top of each row-end st on side edge, *ch 3, dc in next row-end st, ch-2**, dc in next row-end st; rep from * across, ending last rep at **, sk next row-end st, dc in the closest sl st in last row of Back Knee Ribbing, Ldc in each of next 5 sl sts, turn—28 ch-sp; 104 sts. *Note: If you lengthened or shortened the Pineapple Motif, you will have more or fewer sts (in multiples of 7) now and throughout.*

ROWS 1–5: Ch 1, sl st in blo of each st across, turn—104 sts.

ROW 6: Ch 3 (does not count as a st), Ldc in first 2 sts, (make an additional Ldc if you added or subtracted an odd total number of sts to adjust length), *ch 1, sk next st, dc in next st; rep from * across to last 5 sts, Ldc in each of next 5 sts, turn—104 sts with 48 ch-1 sps.

ROWS 7–12: Rep Rows 1–6.

ROWS 13–15: Rep Rows 1–3.

Work series of short rows as follows: [Ch 1, sl st in blo of next 4 sts, turn] twice, [ch 1, sl st in blo of next 8 sts, turn] twice, [ch 1, sl st in blo of next 12 sts, turn] twice, [ch 1, sl st in blo of next 16 sts, turn] twice.

ROW 16 (RS): Rep Row 1.

Fasten off.

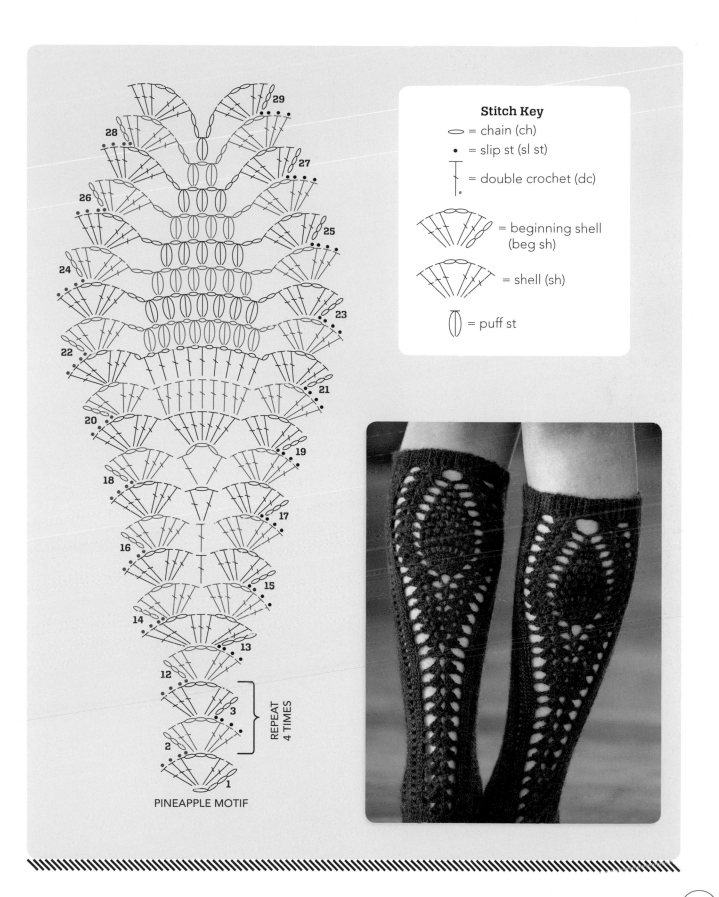

29

28

27

26

25

24

23

22

21

20

19

18

17

16

15

14

13

12

REPEAT 4 TIMES

3

2

1

PINEAPPLE MOTIF

Stitch Key

◯ = chain (ch)

• = slip st (sl st)

🇹 = double crochet (dc)

= beginning shell (beg sh)

= shell (sh)

◍ = puff st

Continue Left Side

With smaller hook, with WS facing, pick up dropped lp on left side of Motif.

ROWS 1–5: Ch 1, sl st in blo of each st across, turn—104 sts.

ROW 6: Ch 3 (does not count as a st), 6 Ldc, ch 1, sk next st, *dc in next st, ch 1, sk next st; rep from * across until 3 sts remain, dc in next st, Ldc in last st, turn—104 sts with 48 ch-1 sps.

Note: If you lengthened or shortened calf you will have more or fewer ch-1 sps.

Note: If you have added or subtracted an odd number of sts (7 for example) you will work until there are 2 sts left, dc in next st, 1 Ldc in last st.

ROWS 7–12: Rep Rows 1–6.

ROWS 13–14: Rep Rows 1–2.

Work series of short rows as follows: [Ch 1, sl st in blo of next 4 sts, turn] twice, [ch 1, sl st in blo of next 8 sts, turn] twice, [ch 1, sl st in blo of next 12 sts, turn] twice, [ch 1, sl st in blo of next 16 sts, turn] twice.

ROW 15 (WS): Rep Row 1.

ROW 16 (RS): Ch 1, sl st in blo of each st across. Connect Sole as follows: Hold Sole so that RS is facing. Starting with the marked st, work sl st in blo of next 44 sts, turn—148 sts total.

Note: St count will be more or less if you lengthened or shortened the calf or foot—keep this in mind throughout the rest of pattern.

ROW 17: Ch 1, sl st in blo of each st across—148 sts.

ROW 18: Ch 3 (does not count as a st), Ldc in each of first 6 sts, ch 1, sk next st, *dc in next st, ch 1, sk next st; rep from * across until only 3 sts remain, dc in next st, Ldc in each of next 2 sts, turn—70 ch-1 sps with a total of 147 sts. If you lengthened or shortened calf, you will have more or fewer (dc, ch-1, sk 1) reps. If you have added or subtracted an odd number of sts (7 for example), you will work until there are 2 sts left, dc in next st, Ldc in last st.

ROWS 19–23: Ch 1, sl st in blo of each st across—148 sts.

ROWS 24-41 (47, 53): Repeat rows 18–23 (3 [4, 5] times).

ROWS 42–43 (48–49, 54–55): Rep Rows 18–19.

Do not fasten off. Place st marker in working loop to keep work from unraveling.

Spray block to measurements and allow to dry completely.

Side Seam

With WS facing, fold stocking lengthwise so that the row with the working lp is in row behind and at the right. Foundation edge of sole should be in front of work, as well as the last row of Right Side. Hold edges together and work in both sets of sts at the same time. Sl st the side seam of stocking, working only through the blo of each st—148 sl sts. Fasten off.

Heel

Hold stocking so that the toe is pointing downward, and you are looking at the back of the foot where the heel would go. There are 36 grooves across the sole edge of heel opening.

SET-UP RND: Using smaller hook and working across the sole edge of opening, insert smaller hook in groove at right corner of heel and pull up loop, ch 1; starting with this same groove, make 36 sc sts across this edge of heel opening to corner of heel opening. Rotate to work across ankle edge of heel. Sc in next 6 grooves,

pm in first of these 6 sc, [2 sc in the side of next dc, sc in next 2 grooves] twice, 2 sc in side of next dc, 3 sc in next row-end st (ending at center back of ankle), 3 sc in next row-end st of sh, 2 sc in side of next dc, [sc in next 2 grooves, 2 sc in next row-end dc] twice, sc in next 6 grooves ending at corner of heel, sl st in first sc of rnd to join—36 sts across bottom of heel opening, 38 sts across top of heel opening—74 sts.

RND 1: Ch 2 (does not count as a st here and throughout), esc2tog (see Glossary) twice, esc (see Glossary) in next 28 sts, esc2tog 4 times, esc in next 30 sts, esc2tog twice, sl st in first st of rnd to join—66 sts.

RND 2: Ch 2, esc2tog, esc in next 28 sts, esc2tog twice, esc in next 30 sts, esc2tog, sl st in first st of rnd to join—62 sts.

RND 3: Ch 2, esc2tog, esc in next 26 sts, esc2tog twice, esc in next 28 sts, esc2tog, sl st in first st of rnd to join—58 sts.

RND 4: Ch 2, esc2tog twice, esc in next 20 sts, esc2tog 4 times, esc in next 22 sts, esc2tog twice, sl st in first st of rnd to join—50 sts.

RND 5: Ch 2, esc2tog, esc in next 20 sts, esc2tog twice, esc in next 22 sts, esc2tog, sl st in first st of rnd to join—46 sts.

RND 6: Ch 2, esc2tog, esc in next 18 sts, esc2tog twice, esc in next 20 sts, esc2tog, sl st in first st of rnd to join—42 sts.

RND 7: Ch 2, esc2tog twice, esc in next 12 sts, esc2tog 4 times, esc in next 14 sts, esc2tog twice, sl st in first st of rnd to join—34 sts.

RND 8: Ch 2, esc2tog, esc in next 12 sts, esc2tog twice, esc in next 14 sts, esc2tog, sl st in first st of rnd to join—30 sts.

RND 9: Ch 2, esc2tog, esc in next 10 sts, esc2tog twice, esc in next 12 sts, esc2tog, sl st in first st of rnd to join—26 sts.

RND 10: Ch 2, esc2tog, esc in next 8 sts, esc2tog 3 times, esc in next 6 sts, esc2tog twice, sl st in first st of rnd to join—20 sts.

Fasten off, leaving long tail.

Toe

SET-UP RND FOR TOE: Fold Toe end of foot flat. Hold stocking so that the toe opening is pointing upward. With smaller hook, join yarn with sl st in 2nd (3rd, 4th) groove to the right of the sl st seam, ch 1, starting in the same groove, sc in next 2 (3, 4) grooves, (2 sc in next row-end dc, sc in the 2 grooves in next sl st section) 3 (4, 5) times, 2 sc in next row-end dc, sc in next 3 (4, 5) grooves, pm in sc just made, sc in next 19 (21, 23) grooves, join with sl st in first sc—42 (46, 50) sts.

RND 1: Ch 2, starting with the same st as join, now and throughout, esc2tog, 1 esc in each of next 18 (20, 22) sts, esc2tog, 1 esc in each of next 20 (22, 24) sts, join with sl st in first esc—40 (44, 48) sts.

RND 2: Ch 2, [esc2tog, esc in next 16 (18, 20) sts, esc2tog] twice, join with sl st in first esc—36 (40, 44) sts.

RND 3: Ch 2, [esc2tog, esc in next 14 (16, 18) sts, esc2tog] twice, join with sl st in first esc—32 (36, 40) sts.

RND 4: Ch 2, [esc2tog, esc in next 12 (14, 16) sts, esc2tog] twice, join with sl st in first esc—28 (32, 36) sts.

RND 5: Ch 2, [esc2tog, esc in next 10 (12, 14) sts, esc2tog] twice, join with sl st in first esc—24 (28, 32) sts.

RND 6: Ch 2, [esc2tog (twice), esc in next 4 (6, 8) sts, esc2tog (twice)] twice, join with sl st in first esc—16 (20, 24) sts. Fasten off Size S only, leaving a long tail.

Sizes M and L Only

RND 7: Ch 2, [esc2tog (twice), esc in next 2 (4) sts, esc2tog (twice)] twice, join with sl st in first esc—12 (16) sts.

Fasten off, leaving a long tail.

Finishing

Fold heel and toe along decreases to match up open edges. Using yarn tails and yarn needle, sew seams in toe and heel, weaving yarn back and forth through just the front loops. Weave in ends. Block.

Finished Size

Directions are given for size S/M. Changes for L/XL are in parentheses.

Belt measures 2½" wide × 36 (41)" long (6.5 × 91.5 [104] cm). Sample made in size S/M.

Yarn

DK weight (#3 Light).

Shown here: Hemp for Knitting allhemp6Lux (100% hemp; 143 yd [130 m]/3½ oz [100 g]): #60 olive, 3 (4) skeins. Yarn distributed by Lanaknits Designs.

Hooks

Sizes G/6 (4 mm) and E/4 (3.5 mm). *Adjust hook sizes if necessary to obtain correct gauge.*

Notions

Yarn needle; large belt buckle (at least 2" [5 cm]). It's helpful to have the kind where the bar is at one end instead of in the middle of the buckle.

Gauge

With smaller hook, 8 sts = 2" (5 cm). Precise gauge is not critical to this project.

Haute Hippie
BELT

Braided I-cord gives this statement belt incredible texture, and though it looks complicated, it's really very simple! It's also endlessly customizable. Wear it high on the body at the true waist, or make it longer and wear it slung low on your hips. Crochet it with three strands of I-cord instead of five for a narrower belt. Use a vintage belt buckle for a one-of-a-kind piece only you could have created!

DESIGNED BY *Beth Nielsen*

Stitch Guide

I-cord

With larger hook, ch 3, join with sl st to form ring.

Rnd 1: Ch 2 (counts as hdc), 5 hdc in ring—6 hdc. Do not ch or join. Work in a spiral.

Rnd 2: Hdc in each hdc around—6 hdc.

Rep Rnd 2 continuously for desired length. This will create a tight tube that continues to spiral upward.

Last Row: Sc in next hdc, sl st in next hdc. Fasten off.

Braiding 5 Strands: Braiding 5 strands is just like braiding 3 strands, but you go over 2 strands instead of 1 each time. *Take the far right strand, cross it over 2 strands to place it in the middle, and then take the far left strand, cross it over 2 strands to place it in the middle; rep from *.

Belt

Make 5 strands of I-cord 47" (54") (119.5 [137] cm) long. Fasten off.

With yarn needle and yarn, sew beg ends of each I-cord together adjacent to each other in a line. Anchor joined end of I-cords. Braid 5 strands together for length of I-cords. Make sure all I-cords are the same length. You may need to unravel a few cords to make them the proper length. Sew ends together to hold braid in place, forming a nice point at the end.

Edging

RND 1: With smaller hook, join yarn with sl st at beg end of braid (flat end), ch 1, sc across beg edge of braid, work 3 sc in corner st, working 2–3 sc in one strand of I-cord, and then jump to next I-cord as the braid forms; sc down the length of the braid, work 3 sc in point end in same manner, sc up the other side of the braid, work 2 more sc in corner st, join with sl st in first sc.

RND 2: Ch 1, sc in each sc around, working 3 sc in center sc of each corner and in point at end of Belt, join with sl st in first sc.

RND 3: Ch 1, working from left to right, rev sc in each sc around, join with sl st in first rev sc to join. Fasten off.

Finishing

Place bar of buckle at flat end of braid, fold edge of braid over, and sew in place with yarn needle. Weave in ends.

Belt Band (optional)

With smaller hook, ch 35, join with sl st to form ring.

RND 1 (RS): Ch 1, sc in each ch around, sl st in first sc—35 sc.

RND 2: Ch 2 (does not count as a st), hdc in each sc around, join with sl st in first hdc.

RND 3: Ch 1, sc in each hdc around, join with sl st in first sc.

RND 4: Ch 1, working from left to right, rev sc in each sc around, sl st in first rev sc. Fasten off.

EDGING RND: With RS facing, working across opposite side of foundation ch, join yarn with sl st in any ch, ch 1, working from left to right, rev sc in each ch around, sl st in first rev sc. Fasten off. Weave in ends. Slip band onto belt and tack in place with yarn needle if desired, or leave loose so it will slide.

LAST ROW

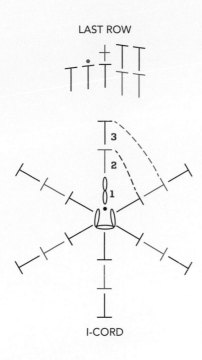

I-CORD

Stitch Key

◯ = chain (ch)

• = slip st (sl st)

+ = single crochet (sc)

T = half double crochet (hdc)

≈+ = reverse sc (rev sc)

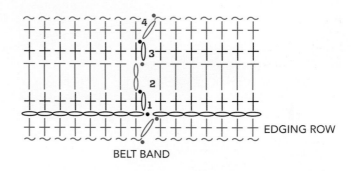

EDGING ROW

BELT BAND

Finished Size

Wrap measures 39 (47)" wide × 15 (18)" long (99 [119.5] × 38 [45.5] cm).

Yarn

Chunky weight (#5 Bulky)

Shown here: The Fibre Co. Tundra (60% baby alpaca, 30% merino wool, 10% silk; 120 yd [110 m]/3½ oz [100 g]): mink, 4 (4) skeins. Yarn distributed by Kelbourne Woolens.

Hook

Size N-15 (10 mm) (P-17 [12 mm]). *Adjust hook size if necessary to obtain correct gauge.*

Notions

Yarn needle.

Gauge

With appropriate hook size, one motif = about 5 (6)" (12.5 [15] cm) diameter.

Notes

A larger-size wrap is created by using a larger hook and following the same instructions and diagrams. It has more drape and will be longer when it is worn.

All stitches are worked with yarn held doubled. The shawl is constructed by joining motifs together as you go (join-as-you-go method).

Boho Blooms
WRAP

This versatile layering piece is a beautiful play on proportion. The wrap is worked with double strands of a rich, chunky, alpaca-blend yarn in a simple design. The heavier-weight yarn and the asymmetrical shape make this wrap modern. This is also a great introduction to the join-as-you-go method of motif projects.

DESIGNED BY *Yumiko Alexander*

Stitch Guide

3-tr Cluster (3-tr cl): [Yo twice, insert hook in ring, yo, draw up a lp, (yo, draw yarn through 2 lps on hook) twice] 3 times, yo, draw yarn through 4 loops on hook.

4-tr Cluster (4-tr cl): [Yo twice, insert hook in ring, yo, draw up a lp, (yo, draw yarn through 2 lps on hook) twice] 4 times, yo, draw yarn through 5 loops on hook.

First Motif

Ch 6, join with sl st to form ring.

RND 1: Ch 4, 3-tr cl in ring, ch 5, [4-tr cl, ch 5] 5 times in ring, join with sl st in first cluster. Fasten off.

Joining Motif in One Loop

Ch 6, join with sl st to form ring.

RND 1: Ch 4, 3-tr cl in ring, ch 5, [4-tr cl, ch 5] 4 times in ring, 4-tr cl in ring, ch 2, sl st in corresponding ch-5 loop of previous motif, ch 2, join with sl st in first cluster. Fasten off.

Joining Motif in Two Loops

Ch 6, join with sl st to form ring.

RND 1: Ch 4, 3-tr cl in ring, ch 5, [4-tr cl, ch 5] 3 times in ring, [4-tr cl in ring, ch 2, sl st in corresponding ch-5 loop of previous motif, ch 2] twice, join with sl st in first cluster. Fasten off.

Wrap

Make First Motif. Make 17 more Motifs; join to previous Motif(s) following Assembly Diagram for placement.

Finishing

Weave in ends.

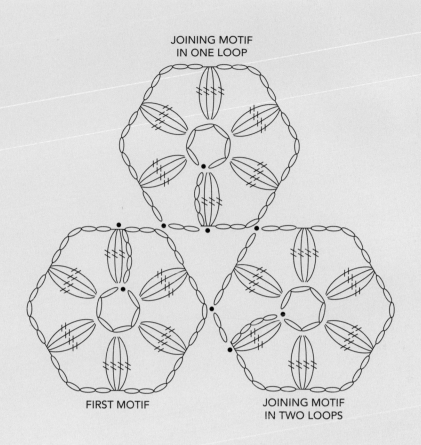

JOINING MOTIF
IN ONE LOOP

FIRST MOTIF

JOINING MOTIF
IN TWO LOOPS

Stitch Key

 = chain (ch)

• = slip st (sl st)

 = 3-tr cluster (3-tr cl)

= 4-tr cluster (4-tr cl)

ASSEMBLY DIAGRAM

Finished Size

Cowl: S/M (M/L) measures 23½ (26½)" (59.5 [67.5] cm) in circumference and 8¼" (21 cm) long. Sample shown in size S/M.

Mittens: S/M (M/L), hand circumference above thumb measures 6½ (7½)" (16.5 [19] cm) and is 8 (9)" (20.5 [23] cm) long. Sample shown in size S/M.

Yarn

Worsted weight (#4 Medium).

Shown here: Grignasco Knits Loden (50% virgin wool, 25% alpaca, 25% viscose; 120 yd [110 m]/1¾ oz [50 g]): #732, cowl 2 (3) skeins; mittens 1 (2) skeins. Yarn distributed by Plymouth Yarn Company.

Hook

Size G/6 (4 mm). *Adjust hook size if necessary to obtain correct gauge.*

Notions

Yarn needle; stitch markers; four ⁵⁄₁₆" (8 mm) black buttons; sewing needle and black sewing thread.

Gauge

17 sts and 8 rows = 4" (10 cm) in dc blo.

Notes

Cowl is worked in the round from the top down.

On the Mittens, the thumbs are made first. Then mitten is worked from fingertip down to webbing of the hand, thumb is attached, and mitten is worked down to cuff in one piece.

Charlie the Owl
COWL & MITTENS

My mother has a fabulously kitschy macramé plant holder adorned with beaded owls that she got in the seventies. Growing up with it in our house, I've always associated owls with Bohemianism. With the resurgence of owls in pop culture, I knew that I had to include them in this collection in some way. Designer Anastasia Popova obliged with this adorable cowl and mitten set.

DESIGNED BY *Anastasia Popova*

Stitch Guide
Front Post Half Treble Crochet (FPhtr)

Yo (twice), insert hook from front to back to front around the post of the corresponding st below, yo and pull up lp, yo and draw through two lps on hook, yo and draw through all lps on hook.

Owl Pattern (worked over 8 sts)

ROW 1: Sk next st, (FPhtr, dc) in next st, dc in next st, working in front of FPhtr just made, FPtr (see Glossary) in same st as FPhtr was worked (ear made), sk next 3 sts, FPtr in next st, dc in last skipped st, working in front of FPtr just made, (dc, FPhtr) in same st as FPtr was worked (ear made), sk next st.

ROW 2: FPhtr in each of next 8 sts.

ROW 3: Sk next 2 sts, FPtr in each of next 2 sts, working in front of post st just made, FPtr in each of last 2 skipped sts, sk next 2 sts, FPtr in next 2 sts, working behind post sts just made, FPtr in each of last 2 skipped sts.

ROWS 4–6: FPhtr in each of next 8 sts.

ROW 7: Rep Row 3.

Rep Rows 2–7 for pattern.

Cowl

RND 1 (RS): Fdc (see Glossary) 100 (112).

RNDS 2–3: Ch 2 (counts as BPdc), *FPdc (see Glossary) in each of next 2 sts, BPdc (see Glossary) in each of next 2 sts; rep from * around to last 3 sts, FPdc in each of next 2 sts, BPdc in next st, join with sl st in top of beg ch-2—100 (112) sts.

Size S/M Only

RND 4: Ch 3, dc in blo of each st around, join with sl st in top of beg ch-3—100 sts.

Size M/L Only

RND 4: Ch 3, dc in blo of each st around to last 3 sts, dc2tog in blo of next 2 sts, dc in blo of last st, join with sl st in top of beg ch-3—111 sts.

All Sizes

RNDS 5–6: Ch 3, dc in blo of each st around, join with sl st in top of beg ch-3—100 (111) sts.

RND 7: Ch 3, *work Row 1 of Owl Pattern over next 8 sts, dc in blo of next 3 sts; rep from * around, sl st in top of ch-3.

RND 8: Ch 3, *work Row 2 of Owl Pattern over next 8 sts, dc in blo of next 3 sts; rep from * around, sl st in top of ch-3.

RND 9: Ch 3, *work Row 3 of Owl Pattern over next 8 sts, dc in blo of next 3 sts; rep from * around, sl st in top of ch-3.

RND 10: Ch 3, *work Row 4 of Owl Pattern over next 8 sts, dc in blo of next 3 sts; rep from * around, sl st in top of ch-3.

RND 11: Ch 3, *work Row 5 of Owl Pattern over next 8 sts, dc in blo of next 3 sts; rep from * around, sl st in top of ch-3.

RND 12: Ch 3, *work Row 6 of Owl Pattern over next 8 sts, dc in blo of next 3 sts; rep from * around, sl st in top of ch-3.

RND 13: Ch 3, *work Row 7 of Owl Pattern over next 8 sts, dc in blo of next 3 sts; rep from * around, sl st in top of ch-3.

RND 14 (WS): Ch 1, sc in each st around, join with sl st in first sc, turn.

RND 15 (RS): Ch 3, *dc in flo of each of next st, dc in blo of each of next 6 sts, dc in flo in each of next 4 sts; rep from * around, join with sl st in top of beg ch-3.

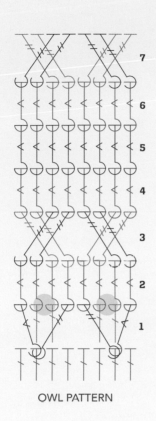

OWL PATTERN

Stitch Key

◯ = chain (ch)

• = slip st (sl st)

⊥ = double crochet (dc)

⊥ = Front Post half treble crochet (FPhtr)

⊥ = Front Post treble crochet (FPtr)

● = positon of button for eye

Size S/M Only

RNDS 16–17: Ch 3, dc in blo of each st around, join with sl st in top of beg ch-3—100 sts.

Size M/L Only

RNDS 16–17: Ch 3, dc in first st (inc made), dc in blo of each st around, join with sl st in top of beg ch-3—112 sts.

All Sizes

RNDS 18–19: Ch 2 (counts as BPdc), *FPdc in each of next 2 sts, BPdc in each of next 2 sts; rep from * around to last 3 sts, FPdc in each of next 2 sts, BPdc in next st, join with sl st in top of beg ch-2—100 (112) sts.

Fasten off. Weave in ends. Block lightly.

𝓣𝓱𝓾𝓶𝓫 (make 2)

RND 1: Make an adjustable ring (see Glossary), ch 3 (counts as dc here and throughout), work 9 (11) dc in ring, join with sl st in top of beg ch-3—10 (12) dc.

RNDS 2–5: Ch 3, dc blo of each st around, sl st in top of ch-3.

Fasten off. Set aside.

𝓡𝓲𝓰𝓱𝓽 𝓜𝓲𝓽𝓽𝓮𝓷

RND 1 (RS): Make an adjustable ring, ch 3 (counts as dc here and throughout), work 11 dc in ring, join with sl st in top of beg ch-3—12 sts.

RND 2: Ch 3, 2 dc in blo of each st around, dc blo of sl st of previous rnd, join with sl st in top of beg ch-3—24 sts.

Size S/M Only

RND 3: Ch 3, [dc in blo of each of next 5 sts, 2 dc in blo of next st] 3 times, dc in blo of each of next 5 sts, dc in blo of sl st of previous rnd, join with sl st in top of beg ch-3—28 sts.

Size M/L Only

RND 3: Ch 3, [dc in blo of each of next 2 sts, 2 dc in blo of next st] 7 times, dc in blo of each of next 2 sts, dc in blo of sl st of previous rnd, join with sl st in top of beg ch-3—32 sts.

All Sizes

RNDS 4–5 (4–6): Ch 3, dc in blo of each st around, join with sl st in top of beg ch-3—28 (32) sts.

RND 6 (7): Ch 3, dc in blo of each of next 9 (11) sts; work Row 1 of Owl Pattern over next 8 sts, dc in blo of each st around, join with sl st in top of beg ch-3.

RND 7 (8): Ch 3, dc in blo of each of next 9 (11) sts; work Row 2 of Owl Pattern over next 8 sts, dc blo of each st around, join with sl st in top of beg ch-3.

RND 8 (9): Ch 3, dc in blo of each of next 9 (11) sts; work Row 3 of Owl Pattern over next 8 sts, dc in blo of each st around, join with sl st in top of beg ch-3.

RND 9 (10): Ch 3, dc in blo of each of next 9 (11) sts; work Row 4 of Owl Pattern over next 8 sts, dc blo of each st around, join with sl st in top of beg ch-3.

RND 10 (11): Ch 3, dc in blo of each of next 9 (11) sts; work Row 5 of Owl Pattern over next 8 sts, dc blo of each st around, join with sl st in top of beg ch-3.

RND 11 (12) (JOIN THUMB): Ch 3, dc in blo of each of next 2 (4) sts; working in next st of mitten and first st of thumb, work dc2tog in blo, dc in blo of each of next 6 (8) sts of thumb, sk next 2 sts of mitten, working in next st of thumb and next st of mitten, work dc2tog in blo, dc in blo of each of next 3 sts; work Row 6 of Owl Pattern over next 8 sts, dc in blo of each st around, join with sl st in top of beg ch-3—32 (38) sts.

RND 12 (13): Ch 3, dc in blo of each of next 2 (4) sts, dc2tog in blo over next 2 sts, dc in blo of each of next 4 (6) sts, dc2tog blo, dc in blo of each of next 3 sts; work Row 7 of Owl Pattern over next 8 sts, dc blo of each st around, join with sl st in top of beg ch-3, turn—30 (36) sts.

RND 13 (14) (WS): Ch 1, sc in each st around, join with sl st in first sc, turn.

RND 14 (15) (RS): Ch 3, dc in flo of each of next 2 (4) sts, dc2tog in flo over next 2 sts, dc in flo of each of next 2 (4) sts, dc2tog in flo over next 2 sts, dc in flo of each of next 3 (4) sts, dc in blo of each of next 6 sts, dc in flo in each st around, join with sl st in top of beg ch-3—28 (34) sts.

Size M/L Only

RND 16: Ch 3, dc in blo of each of next 4 sts, dc2tog in blo over next 2 sts, dc in blo of each of next 2 sts, dc2tog in blo over next 2 sts, dc blo of each st around, join with sl st in top of beg ch-3—32 sts.

All Sizes

RNDS 15–16 (17–18): Ch 3, dc in blo of each st around, join with sl st in top of beg ch-3.

RNDS 17–18 (19–20): Ch 2, *FPdc in each of next 2 sts, BPdc in each of next 2 sts; rep from * around to last 3 sts, FPdc in each of next 2 sts, BPdc in next st, join with sl st in top of beg ch-2.

Fasten off. Weave in ends.

Left Mitten

Work same as Right Mitten through Rnd 10 (11).

RND 11 (12) (JOIN THUMB): Ch 3, dc in blo of each of next 9 (11) sts, work Row 6 of Owl Pattern over next 8 sts, dc in blo of each of next 2 (4) sts, working in next st of mitten and first st of thumb, work dc2tog in blo, dc in blo of next 6 (8) sts of thumb, sk next 2 sts of mitten, working in next st of thumb and next st of mitten, work dc2tog in blo, dc in blo of each st around, join with sl st in top of beg ch-3—32 (38) sts.

RND 12 (13): Ch 3, dc in blo of each of next 9 (11) sts; work Row 7 of Owl Pattern over next 8 sts, dc in blo of each of next 2 (4) sts, dc2tog in blo over next 2 sts, dc in blo of each of next 4 (6) sts, dc2tog in blo over next 2 sts, dc in blo of each st around, join with sl st in top of beg ch-3, turn—30 (36) sts.

RND 13 (14) (WS): Ch 1, sc in each st around, join with sl st in first sc, turn.

RND 14 (15) (RS): Ch 3, dc in flo of each of next 10 (12) sts, dc in blo of each of next 6 sts, dc in flo of each of next 3 (5) sts, dc2tog in flo over next 2 sts, dc in flo of each of next 2 (4) sts, dc2tog in flo over next 2 sts, dc in flo in each st around, join with sl st in top of beg ch-3—28 (34) sts.

Size M/L Only

RND 16: Ch 3, dc in blo of each of next 23 sts, dc2tog in blo over next 2 sts, dc in blo in each of next 2 sts, dc2tog in blo over next 2 sts, dc in blo of each st around, join with sl st in top of beg ch-3—32 sts.

All Sizes

Complete same as Right Mitten.

Finishing

Block lightly. Using yarn needle, sew the gap between thumb and mitten. With sewing needle and thread, sew 2 buttons in Rnd 6 of each mitten at base of each ear in Owl Pattern.

Abbreviations

beg begin(s); beginning

bet between

CC contrasting color

ch(s) chain(s)

cl(s) cluster(s)

cm centimeter(s)

cont continue(s); continuing

dc double crochet

dec decrease(s); decreasing; decreased

dtr double treble (triple)

est established

foll follows; following

g gram(s)

hdc half double crochet

inc increase(s); increasing; increased

lp(s) loop(s)

m marker; meter

MC main color

mm millimeter(s)

p picot

patt pattern(s)

pm place marker

rem remain(s); remaining

rep repeat; repeating

rev sc reverse single crochet

rnd(s) round(s)

RS right side

sc single crochet

sl slip

sl st slip(ped) stitch

sp(s) space(s)

st(s) stitch(es)

tch turning chain

tog together

tr treble crochet

WS wrong side

yd yard(s)

yo yarn over

* repeat starting point

() alternate measurements and/or instructions; work instructions within parentheses in place directed

[] work bracketed instructions a specified number of times

Glossary

Chain (ch)

Make a slipknot and place it on crochet hook. *Yarn over hook and draw through loop on hook. Repeat from * for the desired number of stitches.

Double Crochet (dc)

*Yarn over hook, insert hook in a stitch, yarn over hook and draw up a loop (3 loops on hook; **figure 1**), yarn over hook and draw it through 2 loops (**figure 2**), yarn over hook and draw it through remaining 2 loops on hook (**figure 3**). Repeat from *.

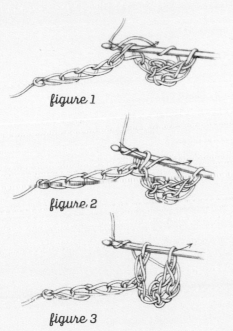

figure 1

figure 2

figure 3

Half Double Crochet (hdc)

*Yarn over, insert hook in stitch (**figure 1**), yarn over and pull up loop (3 loops on hook), yarn over (**figure 2**) and draw through all loops on hook (**figure 3**); repeat from *.

figure 1

figure 2

figure 3

Treble Crochet (tr)

*Wrap yarn around hook twice, insert hook in next indicated stitch, yarn over hook and draw up a loop (4 loops on hook; **figure 1**), yarn over hook and draw it through 2 loops (**figure 2**), yarn over hook and draw it through next 2 loops, yarn over hook and draw it through remaining 2 loops on hook (**figure 3**). Repeat from *.

figure 1

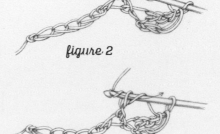

figure 2

figure 3

Making an Adjustable Ring

Make a large loop with the yarn (*figure 1*). Holding the loop with your fingers, insert hook in loop and pull working yarn through loop (*figure 2*). Yarn over hook, pull through loop on hook. Continue to work indicated number of stitches in loop (*figure 3*; shown in single crochet). Pull on yarn tail to close loop (*figure 4*).

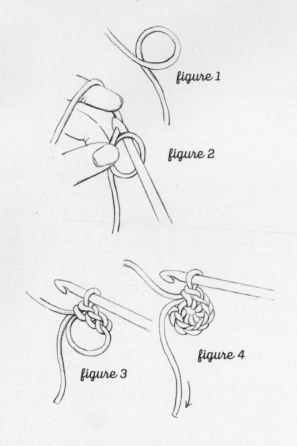

figure 1

figure 2

figure 3

figure 4

Back Post Double Crochet (BPdc)

Yarn over hook, insert hook from back to front to back again around the post of stitch indicated, yarn over hook, draw yarn through stitch, [yarn over hook, draw yarn through 2 loops on hook] twice.

Back Post Half Double Crochet (BPhdc)

Yarn over hook, insert hook from back to front to back around post of corresponding stitch below, yarn over and pull up loop, yarn over hook and draw through all 3 loops on hook.

Back Post Single Crochet (BPsc)

Insert hook from back to front, right to left, around the post of the specified stitch, yarn over hook, pull through work only, yarn over hook, and pull through both loops on hook—1 BPsc made.

Blindstitch

Slide threaded yarn needle in piece A for about ¼" (6 mm). *Poke the needle back out and directly in piece B. Repeat from * until needle is full of stitches, and then pull needle through until yarn is taut. Repeat around, snaking your needle back and forth between the two pieces. Your stitches should be hidden if done correctly.

Double Crochet Two Together (dc2tog)

[Yarn over, insert hook in next stitch, yarn over and pull up loop, yarn over, draw through two loops] twice, yarn over, draw through all loops on hook.

Double Treble Crochet (dtr)

*Yarn over hook three times, insert hook in a stitch, yarn over hook and draw up a loop (5 loops on hook). [Yarn over hook and draw it through 2 loops] 4 times. Repeat from *.

Extended Single Crochet (esc)

Insert hook in next stitch, yarn over hook, draw up a loop (2 loops on hook), yarn over hook and draw through first loop on hook, yarn over hook and draw through both loops on hook—1 esc made.

Extended Single Crochet Two Together (esc2tog)

[Insert hook in next stitch, yarn over hook, draw up a loop (2 loops on hook), yarn over hook and draw through first loop on hook] twice, yarn over hook and draw through 3 loops on hook—1 esc2tog made.

Foundation Double Crochet (fdc)

Ch 3, yarn over hook, insert hook in 3rd ch from hook, yarn over hook and draw up a loop (3 loops on hook), yarn over hook, draw yarn through first loop on hook, [yarn over hook and draw through 2 loops] twice—1 fdc made.

*Yarn over hook, insert hook under both loops of ch just made. Yarn over hook and draw up a loop (3 loops on hook), yarn over hook and draw through 1 loop, [yarn over hook and draw through 2 loops] twice. Rep from * for length of foundation.

Front Post Double Crochet (FPdc)

Yarn over hook, insert hook from front to back to front again around post of stitch indicated, yarn over hook and pull up a loop (3 loops on hook), [yarn over hook and draw through 2 loops on hook] twice—1 FPdc made.

Front Post Treble Crochet (FPtr)

Yarn over hook twice, insert hook in specified stitch from front to back, right to left, around the post (or stem). Yarn over hook, pull through work only, *yarn over hook, pull through 2 loops on hook. Rep from * twice—1 FPtr made.

Half Double Crochet Two Together (hdc2tog)

[Yarn over hook, insert hook in next stitch, yarn over hook and pull up loop] twice *(figure 1)*, yarn over hook and draw through all loops on hook *(figures 2 and 3)*—1 stitch decreased.

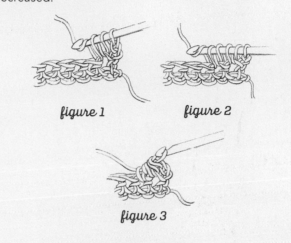

figure 1   *figure 2*

figure 3

Mattress Stitch (mattress st)

With the RS facing, use threaded needle to *bring the needle through the center of the first stitch or post on one piece, and then through the center of the corresponding stitch or post of the other piece. Repeat from * to end of seam.

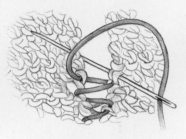

Joining sides of rows.

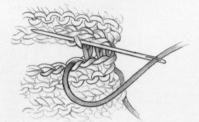

Joining tops of stitches to foundation chain.

Reverse Single Crochet (rev sc)

Working from left to right, *insert hook in next stitch to right, yarn over hook, pull loop through, yarn over hook, pull through both loops on hook; rep from *.

Single Crochet Seam (sc seam)

Place the pieces together with the wrong (WS) or right sides (RS) facing, depending on whether you want your seam to be hidden on the wrong side or show on the right side of your work. Hold the pieces in your hand with the two edges facing you.

Insert the hook through both pieces at the beg of the seam and pull up loop, chain 1. Work a row of single crochet by inserting your hook through both pieces at the same time. Complete the seam and secure the end of the seaming yarn.

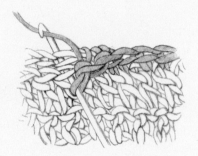

Single Crochet Two Together (sc2tog)

Insert hook in stitch and draw up a loop. Insert hook in next stitch and draw up a loop. Yarn over hook *(figure 1)*. Draw through all three loops on hook *(figures 2 and 3)*—1 stitch decreased.

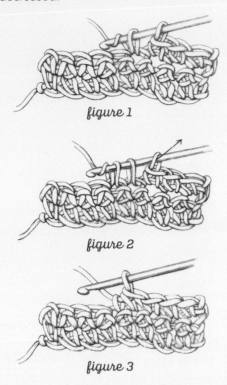

figure 1

figure 2

figure 3

Slip Stitch Seam (sl st seam)

To begin, place a slipknot on a crochet hook. With wrong sides (WS) facing together and working one stitch at a time, *insert crochet hook through both thicknesses in the edge stitches *(figure 1)*, grab a loop of yarn and draw this loop through both thicknesses, and then through the loop on the hook *(figure 2)*.

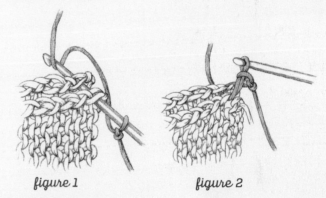

figure 1   *figure 2*

Slip Stitch Embroidery (sl st embroidery aka Ch st embroidery)

Bring threaded needle out from back to front at center of a stitch. Form a short loop and insert needle back where it came out. Keeping the loop under the needle, bring needle back out in center of next stitch to the right.

Whipstitch

With right sides (RS) of work facing and working through edge stitches, bring threaded needle out from back to front, along edge of piece.

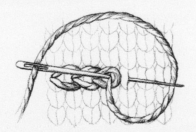

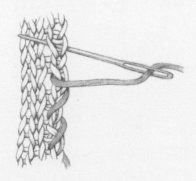

Meet the Contributors

Mimi Alelis has always loved handcrafting and chose crochet as her main hobby for its practical uses and infinite possibilities. She creates and designs what she wants for herself, and for her family and friends. Before the Internet age, she never thought she could find a job doing what she loves. Nowadays she's always thrilled for every design published and every pattern sold. She blogs about her crochet adventures at mycrochetstuff.blogspot.com.

Yumiko Alexander loves clothing and fashion, so her design ideas start with what she wants to have in her closet. She wants her designs to be functional and fashionable, but also very original—not what you might find at a clothing store. She is the author of *Rustic Modern Crochet* (Interweave, 2014).

Shelby Allaho learned to crochet as a child from her grandmother. She really fell in love with the craft when she saw an inspiring collection of modern French crochet in London. After exploring traditional and free-form crochet techniqes, she began designing patterns for various publications. She loves promoting the art of crochet and feels the day is complete when she has created something. She blogs at stitch-story.com.

Brenda K. B. Anderson has been obsessed with making things ever since she can remember. When she was little, Brenda would spend hours making elaborate housing (with trap doors and secret rooms) for her tiny fuzzy bears out of Legos. Even as a little girl she realized the infinite possibilities of building something one block (or stitch) at a time. Her book, *Beastly Crochet* (Interweave), was published in 2013.

Robyn Chachula's latest book, *Blueprint Crochet Sweaters* (Interweave, 2013) tries to take the mystery out of creating custom crochet sweaters. Robyn fell in love with crochet from her first lacy motif and has been designing everything she can from sweaters to lamps ever since. She is incredibly thankful to be able to design and write from home in Pittsburgh, Pennsylvania, while playing with her little "office assistants." See more of her designs at crochetbyfaye.com.

When knit and crochet designer **Yoko Hatta** (aka Kazekobo) was an art student she really wanted to dress in style, but everything that she liked in the shops was expensive and she had little money, so the practice of making her own clothes became a habit. She made pantaloons, knitted sweaters, bags, hats… Now, although she may not always wear the clothes that she designs, her approach is essentially the same. She still likes to pick up new techniques and likes to think first and foremost about what something feels like to wear. See more of her work at kazekobo.net.

Kathy Merrick taught herself to crochet from books and pictures. She sees new things, new details, and fascinating ideas every day in her work. Crocheting feeds her endless curiosity about what happens if you add two more colors or if there is a way to connect motifs without big holes or how many ways can you put these chosen elements together. Along with what happens if you add ten more colors!

Cristina Mershon is a graphic designer by day and crocheter by night. She was born in Spain, in the small region of Galicia, where handcrafting has been a tradition for centuries. She loves creating classic crochet pieces with a modern twist, simple and flattering shapes, and elaborate edgings.

Irish designer **Aoibhe Ni** was taught to crochet by her mam at around the age of twelve. After art college and several successful years as a graphic designer, the recession required a sudden change of direction, and she began selling patterns online. She hasn't looked back since. Aoibhe has been published many times in magazines, teaches regularly in local yarn shops in Dublin and around Ireland, and is currently writing her second e-book of Tunisian-lace shawl patterns. Visit her website at aoibheni.com.

After experimenting in various aspects of the fashion industry, Chicago-based designer **Beth Nielsen** began her obsession with crochet and her fascination with fashion to design crochet patterns for various publications. She seeks to create fashion-forward crocheted garments and accessories with a fresh, modern perspective. Visit her at chicrochet.com for more of her patterns and video tutorials.

Annette Petavy's recipe for crochet-designer cake: take one heaping cup of Swedish upbringing, in a family where different types of needle arts were practiced by almost every woman. Add an equal amount of living in France, where aesthetics and style are part of daily life. Combine thoroughly, pouring in lavish amounts of fascination for the unexplored possibilities of crochet. Bake until you consider done. Eat, preferably in the garden with a big cup of tea.

Anastasia Popova is a contributor to the soon-to-be-published *Fresh Design Crochet* book series by Cooperative Press. Her crochet career began when she designed and produced a line of kids' clothes and accessories for local boutiques. Catch up with Anastasia at anastasiapopova.com.

Sarah Read is the technical editor for *Interweave Crochet*. When she's not stitching or playing Legos with her son, she's reading and writing. Sometimes she even sleeps a little.

Natasha Robarge learned to crochet when she was a child. She first loved the process of making something, and then later loved the products of her work because she could wear them or use them in her home. Now, she loves to transform ideas into crochet designs. She wonders what other great things crochet has in store for her! Find out more about her at aperfectloop.com.

Linda Skuja is the designer behind the indie crochet pattern brand Eleven Handmade. She designs modern and edgy garments and accessories for young adults and those who feel young at heart. Linda is taking crochet to another level by focusing on simple stitches that result in eye-catching creations. She has received multiple awards and created garments for the runway of New York Fashion Week in 2012. Check out her blog, Eleven Handmade Crochets, at lindaskuja.com.

Jill Wright was taught to crochet at the age of eight by a neighbor in England. Jill has always loved all kinds of crafts, so crochet was a natural extension of her skills. Pros for crochet include: you only have to control one stitch at any time; it's easy to rip out (unless you're working with laceweight mohair); and crocheted lace looks amazing! Designing crochet pieces now offers a welcome break between knitwear designs. If it involves yarn, Jill will try it.

Acknowledgments

I want to sincerely thank everyone at Interweave for believing in the vision I had for a truly chic crochet collection, but especially Karin Strom, Allison Korleski, and Marcy Smith. Thank you to the editorial, photography, design, and production teams who helped make the vision a reality, including Michelle Bredeson, Karen Manthey, Joe Hancock, Julia Boyles, Adrian Newman, and Katherine Jackson.

A big heap of crochet gratitude to the designers: Mimi Alelis, Yumiko Alexander, Shelby Allaho, Brenda K. B. Anderson, Robyn Chachula, Yoko Hatta, Kathy Merrick, Cristina Mershon, Aoibhe Ni, Beth Nielsen, Annette Petavy, Anastasia Popova, Sarah Read, Natasha Robarge, Linda Skuja, and Jill Wright. I had a concept, but you all made it beautifully real. Your projects were not only the talk of the Interweave offices, but they exceeded my greatest expectations.

Much gratitude is due to the yarn companies who provided all the amazing fibers that elevated each and every project on these pages: Berroco, Blue Sky Alpacas, Brown Sheep Co., Cascade Yarns, Classic Elite Yarns, Dream in Color, Fyberspates, Kelbourne Woolens, Lanaknits Designs, Louet, Madelinetosh, Malabrigo, Fairmount Fibers, Knitting Fever, Plymouth Yarn, Quince & Co., Skacel, Tahki-Stacy Charles Inc., Universal Yarn, and WEBS.

Finally, thank you to my family and friends who endured countless conversations about crochet and yarn, and perhaps a few too many celebratory dances around the living room as projects arrived at my doorstep.

Resources

Yarns

Berroco
1 Tupperware Dr., Ste. 4
N. Smithfield, RI 02896
(401) 769-1212
berroco.com

Blue Sky Alpacas
PO Box 88
Cedar, MN 55011
(763) 753-5815
blueskyalpacas.com

**Brown Sheep
Company, Inc.**
100662 County Rd. 16
Mitchell, NE 69357
(800) 826-9136
brownsheep.com

Cascade Yarns
1224 Andover Park E.
Tukwila, WA 98188
(206) 574-0440
cascadeyarns.com

Classic Elite Yarns
122 Western Ave.
Lowell, MA 01851
classiceliteyarns.com

Dream in Color
907 Atlantic Ave.
West Chicago, IL 60185
dreamincoloryarn.com

**The Fibre Company/
Kelbourne Woolens**
2000 Manor Rd.
Conshohocken, PA 19428
(484) 368-3666
kelbournewoolens.com

Fyberspates Ltd
fyberspates.co.uk

**Grignasco/
Plymouth Yarn**
500 Lafayette St.
Bristol, PA 19007
(215) 788-0459
plymouthyarn.com

**Hempforknitting/
Lanaknits Designs**
Suite 3B, 320 Vernon St.
Nelson, BC
Canada V1L 4E4
(888) 301-0011
lanaknits.com

Louet North America
3425 Hands Rd.
Prescott, ON
Canada K0E 1T0
(613) 925-4502
louet.com

Madelinetosh
7515 Benbrook Pkwy.
Benbrook, TX 76126
(817) 249-3066
madelinetosh.com

Malabrigo
(786) 866-6187
malabrigoyarn.com

**Manos del Uruguay/
Fairmount Fibers**
915 N. 28th St.
Philadelphia, PA 19130
(888) 566-9970
fairmountfibers.com

**Mirasol Yarns/
Knitting Fever**
PO Box 336
315 Bayview Ave.
Amityville, NY 11701
(516) 546-3600
knittingfever.com

Misti Alpaca
PO Box 2532
Glen Ellyn, IL 60138
(888) 776-9276
mistialpaca.com

Quince and Co.
32 Main St., Ste. 13-101W
Biddeford, ME 04005
quinceandco.com

Shibui Knits
1500 NW 18th Ave., Ste. 110
Portland, OR 97209
(503) 595-5898
shibuiknits.com

Tahki Yarns
70-60 83rd St., Bldg. #12
Glendale, NY 11385
(800) 338-YARN
tahkistacycharles.com

Universal Yarn
5991 Caldwell Park Dr.
Harrisburg, NC 28075
(877) 864-9276
universalyarn.com

**Valley Yarns/
WEBS**
6 Industrial Pkwy.
Easthampton, MA 01027
(800) 367-9327
yarn.com

**Zitron/
Skacel Knitting, Inc.**
PO Box 88110
Seattle, WA 98138
(800) 255-1278
skacelknitting.com

Notions

Casa Batlló Cloche

BUTTONS ("JOLYN")

Lots of Buttons
lotsofbuttons.com

Chrysanthemum Capelet

BUTTONS

M&J Trimming
mjtrim.com

Gypsy Slouch

BEADS

Bead in Hand
beadinhand.com

Haute Hippie Belt

BUCKLE

Similar styles are available at nonickel.com

Petula Purse

MAGNETIC SNAPS, D-RINGS, AND PURSE STRAP

**Jo-Ann Fabric and
Craft Stores**
joann.com

NEEDLE-FELTING MAT AND PEN-STYLE NEEDLE-FELTING TOOL

Clover USA
clover-usa.com

Purse of Prosperity

PURSE FRAME AND CHAIN STRAP

3Dpatternpaper
*etsy.com/
shop/3Dpatternpaper*

Index

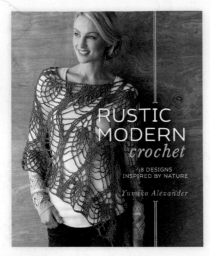

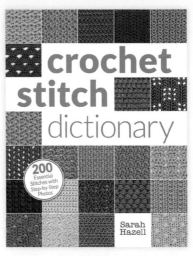